Batons and Bows

The story of

The Tiverton Youth Orchestra

by Ron Davey

Edited by Margaret Davey and Jeanne Kellow

KELLY PUBLICATIONS
6 Redlands, Tiverton,
Devon, EX16 4DH
2002

Acknowledgments

The editors are grateful to the following for permission to reproduce their photographs:

David Chivers (front cover); Castle Photographers; *Tiverton Gazette; Express & Echo; The Guardian*

First published by
KELLY PUBLICATIONS
6 Redlands, Tiverton, Devon EX16 4DH UK
2002

ISBN 1 903053 16 1

Printed by Maslands Ltd, Tiverton, Devon

Contents

At Knightshayes

Foreword

For almost 50 years Ron Davey ran the Tiverton Youth Orchestra which he had founded in 1944.He was still playing in it well after his 80th birthday. For all that time he taught, inspired and probably sometimes goaded generations of young people to learn to play and to enjoy music. His great sense of fun and his infectious ability to inspire others were two of the factor that ensured the orchestra's success.

We are fortunate that we can share his memories through this book which is a wonderful chronicle of the history of a unique part of Tiverton's community.

Sir Ian Amory, Bt (2002)

A Tiverton Youth Orchestra concert — 1987

How I Became Interested in Music

Without music, life would be a mistake

(Nietzche)

I suppose, if I am to start at the very beginning, I must go back to a day in 1919, when I was seven years old and a pupil of Heathcoat School, King Street, now the local Community Centre. My Headmaster, Mr R. Woodward, had asked if any boys would like to learn to play a violin and so, in great excitement, I went home to ask my parents if I might do so. At that time I lived at number 10, John Street, my father being a foundryman who became a foreman at the Exeleigh foundry – part of the factory. They agreed that I could have the lessons, which meant some sacrifice on their part as they would have to buy me a violin (which I still have) at a cost of £1.10 shillings and also pay for the lessons at about 3 old pence per week. This may not sound very much, but out of my father's weekly wage of about £2, it was quite a lot. My first teacher was Mr Phil Baker who used to come to the school to give us our lessons. To start with, there was a group of about 8 boys and once we could play a little we used to do so every morning at Assembly. I remember that it was my job to knock at each classroom door to summon the violin boys to the school hall in readiness. Later, the lessons were taught by the Headmaster's daughter, Miss Marjorie Woodward. So began my life-long love of music – especially, of course, the violin.

As I became more proficient I had plenty of opportunities to show off my skills at various concerts, Chapel anniversaries, etc, mostly at the Methodist Church in St Peter Street where my family attended regularly. I was also asked to play at the Memorial Hall on Sunday evenings after the church services where a regular musical concert would be held. In those days there was no radio or TV and the hall would be crowded each week with people eager to be entertained. A quartet would sing, which included Bill Lloyd, Frank Brooks (who also played a violin), Harold Hillman and Fred Reed. Others who took part included Reg Heal (solo bass), who was a local fishmonger and a semi-professional singer; Roland Huish (tenor);

Fred Rendell, another tenor; Albert Walker and many others. I would play a few violin solos.

I also played in just about every church and chapel for miles around, accompanied at the piano by Mr Charlie Poslett, or Norman Stevens who was a local gents' hairdresser, or sometimes Mrs Heal who was at that time the organist at the Methodist Church. Some of the others who would also take part in these programmes were Triffie Martin, who was a fine contralto, Reg Heal and Frank Brooks.

When I was ten years old I felt very honoured to be invited to play in the orchestra that always accompanied the Heathcoat Operatic Society's shows. This was long before the present Tiverton Operatic Society was formed. The Producer and Musical Director was Mr Home Smith who was at that time the principal overseas representative of John Heathcoat & Co. Mr Frank Hamlin was also involved in these productions, and his wife was a very good violinist who also played with this orchestra. He was very friendly with Mr Basil Cameron who would come to stay with him. He used to advise on the production and sometimes conducted. Mr Frank Burch, well known in local musical circles, also began with this Society and the Hon. Leslie Butler used to take many leading roles.

I was the only child in the Orchestra and I rather think a few of the adult players resented my being there! However, I was able to play the music as well as any of them and greatly enjoyed taking part.

After a time, Miss Woodward decided to go abroad to work and I then began having lessons with Mr R. Bareham. I continued my various musical engagements and at the age of 14 years I left school to work at The Tiverton Motor Company in Blundell's Road, learning how to paint cars and other vehicles – but that is another story.

My 'Oxford Education'

The English may not like music,
but they absolutely love the noise it makes

(Sir Thomas Beecham)

Eventually, in 1932, I felt it was time to leave home and spread my wings. I wrote to three firms, who all offered me work, but I decided to go to Oxford where I was offered a post at what was then Morris Motors, owned by Mr William Morris who of course later became Lord Nuffield. I had nine very happy years there and my violin opened many doors for me, to a variety of interesting experiences. When I first arrived in Oxford I knew no one. I had to find lodgings and it took me quite a while to get used to the work. I had never used a paint-sprayer before and although the pay was a lot more than at Tiverton the work was quite hard and the hours long – 8 am till 6 pm plus overtime when required.

I soon got to know people, however, and my foreman in the paint-shop, Ted Rogers, discovering that I liked music, asked if I would like to join a choir to which he belonged. They were about to give a recital of Handel's Messiah at Oxford Town Hall so I went along to a few rehearsals and was allowed to take part. The singers were accompanied at the performance by the Oxford Light Orchestra under Sir Thomas Beecham. Well, I sang all through the first part of the programme but all the time I was enviously eyeing the orchestra and wishing very much that I was down there with them, rather than singing with the choir!

During the interval I managed to mingle with the players and began to chat to some of them. When they heard that I was a violinist they immediately invited me to join them although at that time I didn't have my violin with me in Oxford. Sir Thomas Beecham himself managed to find a spare one for me to borrow and so, when the programme resumed, there I was, merrily bowing away as part of the orchestra and thoroughly enjoying myself, to the amazement of my foreman, who was of course standing back with the choir!

After that I became a regular member of the Oxford Light Orchestra and, with them, took part in numerous engagements in the area. As I settled in to my new life I began to discover that there was a wealth of new experiences available to me and found that I was able to attend many of the lectures that were open to people outside the colleges, as well as recitals by famous musicians and some who, though very good, were not so well known.

One evening I went to Mansfield College to hear a Mr Spicer, who was the college organist and choirmaster, give an organ recital. Afterwards, I chatted to him and his son, who was a cellist. When they heard that I played a violin in the OLO I was invited to join a small group of players who gave recitals locally. We often played music by Leslie Betteridge, a friend of Mr Spicer, which was handwritten and very hard indeed to read! Thus, by degrees, as one might say, I broadened my musical knowledge and also filled in many gaps in my general education, caused by a series of childhood illnesses which had made me miss a great deal of schooling. And all this without being an undergraduate myself!

Sometimes at concerts and recitals I used to find myself sitting next to James Agate, who was at that time a well known music critic for the Oxford Times as well as for one of the big national dailies. He was quite happy to discuss the performances, explaining what to look for, and through his knowledge I developed an insight into how to judge what was good (and not so good) in music.

This very pleasant part of my life came to an end with the outbreak of the Second World War in 1939. My several attempts to join one of the armed forces failed because of my medical history, and my mother was in very poor health, so I decided to return to Tiverton.

The War Years

Tiverton Youth Orchestra 1944

Music is the endeavour of the soul to speak

(Joseph Joachim)

On my return to Tiverton I went to work for R.T. Dart, who had a firm repairing and painting cars, lorries etc, plus sign writing. During this period we were also required to undertake various jobs to do with the war effort, such as painting army equipment and so on. When the Home Guard was formed I was among the first to join and so I became one of 'Dad's Army'. Again, this is another story and I could easily fill another book with memories of those times.

I had discovered on my return to Tiverton that virtually all the music activities I remembered had died out. One evening I had a visit from Mr Bernard Mudford, who was the organist at the Congregational Church in St. Peter St (now the United Reformed Church). He asked if I would play my violin at their forthcoming Anniversary – some hymns and a few tunes with the organ.

At about that time I played a few solos at concerts at Blundell's School and as a result had been approached by a Mrs Sarah Martin whose son Christopher wanted to learn to play the violin. I agreed to give him some lessons, although I had never taught anyone before. I also knew two other boys who could play, another to whom I had taught the double bass and a lad in the Salvation Army who could play a trumpet. Over the next few weeks I managed to gather together about twelve young players and we had a few rehearsals in the Congregational Church rooms. Our pianist for this was Mrs G. Hardwick (née Land), a family connection. We then played for the Anniversary as promised and decided to stay together, rehearsing in the church rooms and giving several small concerts around Tiverton.

The late Viscount Amory, who was then Mr Derrick Amory, began to take an interest in what we were doing and suggested we should call ourselves the Tiverton Youth Orchestra. He became our patron, President and a very good friend from then on.

The original members included Christopher Martin (who was the leader), Ken Greenslade, Brian Greenslade, Alan and Ron Smale, Richard Bowden, Ron Gratton, Charles Land, Fred Grant, George Burt, Trevor Chilcott, Clifford Pinhay, 'Sonny' Venner and Bob Lapworth (piano). Mrs Dorothy Jenkins, whose husband was manager of the local Co-op, also played the piano for us.

At this time I was invited to join a local dance band, *The New Ambassadors,* as a double bass player. We used to play at dances in and around Tiverton and various other local events, and also entertained the troops. The other players included Tom Howe, Norman Stevens, Donald Beer, Eddie Huxham, Roy Rowsell (who I hear later emigrated to Canada) Pat Kirk (whose father had a bookshop) and Fred Loosemore. I also used to play for the Washfield Rhythm Band.

During my absence from Tiverton, Mr Bareham had died and the Heathcoat Operatic Society had given way to the Tiverton Operatic Society. They used to gather a selection of local musicians each year to play for their productions, much the same as they do nowadays, and I used to play the double bass for them.

Very little instrumental music was being taught in schools, although the Heathcoat School in King Street had some violin classes organised by Miss Winifred Kingdom. Blundell's School had a flourishing music department, but in those days the boys were discouraged from having much contact with the town. Our very first engagement was at a fete at Old Blundell's School in aid of the RAF Comforts Fund. I remember the Sea Cadets and the 1079 Squadron Air Cadet Force (under Mr Sam Leaker) also taking part.

Since then, the Tiverton Youth Orchestra has had regular contacts with Blundell's School. As we became better known the number of engagements offered to us increased rapidly. As a result I was asked to accept a few more pupils for violin, cello and double bass lessons at my home, so as you may imagine, my time became fully occupied. Not only did I have the dance bands and the Youth Orchestra, plus my pupils, but also my Home Guard duties, which often required long hours (after

Tiverton Youth Orchestra at the Heathcoat Hall — 1946
Back row: Walt Hoare, Sonny Venner, Phil Williams, Brian Greenslade, Merv Garland, George Burt, Ron Davey, Norman Stevens, Clifford Penhay, Tony Pearce, Trevor Chilcot
Seated: Ronald Smale, Alan Smale, Dick Bowden, Chris Martin, Ken Greenslade, Fred Grant, Cliff Grafton, Alan Shapland, Charlie Land, Bobby Lapworth

working a forty-hour week) and were taken very seriously. I finally had to give up playing for the Operatic Society and the dance bands as my involvement with the Youth Orchestra increased.

In the 1940s, two ladies, Miss Trout and Miss Wolkes, founded the Tiverton Signpost Club for girls and they began their now well-established custom of presenting an annual Christmas pantomime. We were asked to provide the music for this (although they had a regular pianist, Mr Norman Stevens, who had a gentlemen's hairdressing business on the corner of Barrington Street and Lowman Green) and we did this for many years. Later on, as is well known, the club was organised by Mrs Margaret Batting and for a long time all the scripts were written and produced by Mr Reg Elsworthy. I would attend rehearsals, and discussions would take place regarding what music was required for the various songs and dances and incidental music, such as timely drum-rolls, cymbal crashes etc!

We would also play light music during the interval. I would rehearse it all with the Youth Orchestra separately, and near the date of the actual performance we would put it all together.

After Norman Stevens died, the club accompanist for rehearsals was Mr Albert Trout.

Eventually, we had to change our place of rehearsal after a fire in the Congregational Church. Mr Maddocks, headmaster of the Heathcoat Junior School (then next to the Factory), invited us to make use of the school hall, which we did for a number of years. The Devon Education Department heard about the Youth Orchestra and gave us written permission to rehearse there without charge.

We were then asked to provide interval music at the Tiverton Dramatic Society productions – three or four a year – under their producer, Mr Alf Tidball. In addition we were still asked to give concerts at most of the villages in the area and in Exeter.

During the first ten years I was amazed to discover that we had averaged over 50 engagements each year – no wonder I had little spare time! Running a youth organisation of any kind requires a lot of commitment and the orchestra was no exception. At first we had no funds and nobody paid subscriptions, neither did I have any help with the administration. So, out of my own pocket came the cost of sheet music, which I had to choose carefully so that we had a good variety on the programme whilst keeping within our capabilities. I also seemed to be forever supplying spare strings, as players used to break them regularly while trying to tune up.

When we had a concert outside the town, I used to hire a bus from Mr Clatworthy to take the members, while I went on ahead in my car. I would have the drums in the back of the car and the double bass in its leatherette case strapped on the roof in all winds and weathers. There are no prizes for guessing who paid for the bus – not many parents then had cars to help with transport. I had to take all the music stands to rehearsals and concerts as well and sort out all the sheet music before and after each one.

I recall one concert we gave; it must have been in the 1940s, at the Workhouse, which later became Belmont Hospital. There were quite a number of inmates in our audience, maybe about 100. Everyone, including the players, had to sit on very uncomfortable wooden benches. I remember seeing some of the men chopping up sticks in another part of the building, presumably as part of their chores. As far as I can recall, our concert was very much enjoyed and we were given refreshments afterwards.

Christopher Martin: A Talent Discovered

The right way to begin is to pay attention to
the young and make them as good as possible
(Socrates, 470–399 BC)

In the meantime, I had been teaching Christopher Martin as much as I could on the violin. We had bought dozens of studies, solos and sonatas – as wide a range as possible – and listened to recordings of all the great violinists of the day. I began to realise that here was a great talent, which needed more than I could provide in the way of teaching. By now he had left school, and his father had put him to work in the factory. He was not at all happy with the prospect of spending his life there, but his chances of pursuing his dream of a musical career seemed far out of reach. I went to see Mr Derrick Amory and it was decided that I should write to the London College of Music. They invited Chris up for an interview and an audition and we were delighted when he was offered weekly tuition with Mr Angel Grande (a gifted Spanish violinist) at the London College of Music. Mr Amory arranged for his fees and travelling expenses to be paid and some time later Chris was able to transfer to the Royal College of Music where he attended full-time.

Chris Martin – 1948

Chris lived up to all expectations, making excellent progress under such gifted musicians as Henry Holst and Cecil Aronowitz. A series of prestigious appointments followed including the Edinburgh String Quartet, The London Mozart Players, and The English Chamber Orchestra, fulfilling engagements all over the world. Eventually he became senior lecturer in violin at the University of Melbourne, Australia, whilst also featuring as soloist and conductor with various Australian orchestras and ensembles.

First Celebrity Concert: Angel Grande

We are the music-makers
and we are the dreamers of dreams
(Arthur O'Shaughnessy)

Mr Grande was very interested in hearing about my own part in Chris's training, and when I asked if he would consider coming to Tiverton to give a recital for us he readily agreed. By the time a date was arranged Chris was doing his National Service in the army, but was able to be present.

Tiverton Youth Orchestra concert at the Heathcoat Hall with guest artiste Angel Grande, solo violin — December 1948
Back row: Tony Pearce, Keith Butt, Bob Grabham, 'Nanto' Williams, ——, ——, Irvine Bendelow, Tommy Howe, ——, Glen Chilcot, John Fewings
At piano: Mr Willis
Seated: Rod Osmond, Chris Martin, Michael Chidgey, Den Gunter, Phil Williams, Fred Grant, Brian Greenslade, Merv Garland, Don Nichols
Front: Ron Davey

So, we embarked on our first 'Celebrity Concert', which was held on December 9th 1948 at the Heathcoat Hall. This event caused quite a stir in the town, as I cannot recall there ever having been anything quite like it. Lady Amory was present, also the Mayor and Mayoress, Cllr E.G. Pierce and, according to the Tiverton Gazette cutting, which I still have, many other prominent local personages. Also, according to this report, there were 520 people in the audience, though quite how they were all crammed in is hard to imagine! Perhaps fire regulations were not so strict in those days!

Angel Grande gave an impressive virtuoso recital and the orchestra boys were praised for their smart turnout in white shirts and bow ties.

One rather odd feature of the programme was that, apart from the guest soloist and the Youth Orchestra, there was a display of gymnastics, presented by the boys of St Boniface. This was a Boys' Home at Sampford Peverell, and their instructor, Mr Owen Murphy, had trained them to give an excellent performance. Mr Grande remarked that he had never shared a programme with a gym display before! After the concert he stopped to chat to the orchestra boys – and also the gym team, telling them that he had been very keen on physical fitness as a young man. He then gathered everyone round in a large circle while he demonstrated his 'party piece'. He lay down on the floor with a heavy wooden chair in front of him, grasped one of the legs and then slowly rose (lifting the chair), first to a kneeling position then fully standing, still holding the chair leg, until it was above his head. He challenged anyone else to try it, but nobody could, not even Mr Murphy. We were all very impressed, as much by his willingness to perform the trick as his ability to do it.

Also on the programme was a vocal quartet: A. Walker, F. Murch, T. Dunsford and W. Lloyd, accompanied by Mr C. Poslett. John Fewings sang a solo.

Orchestra members at the time were: C. Martin, D. Gunter, P. Williams, R. Osmant, T. Pearce, F. Grant, M. Chidgey (first violins); B. Greenslade, M. Garland, J. Fewings, E. Chilcott, G. Chilcott, I. Bendelow, D. Nicholls, R. Grabham and W. Greenslade (second violins); K. Butt (double bass); Mr P. Willis (piano); Mr T. Howe (drums); Messrs Williams, Lane and Pook (clarinets); Mr J. Land (trombone). The youngest member was William Greenslade, who was eleven years old.

Eventually, members started paying a small subscription per week to help cover the costs but we never charged any organisation for our concerts and rarely gave one for our own benefit.

Loyal Supporters

Whosoever loves much, performs much and
can accomplish much.
What is done in love, is well done.

(Vincent Van Gogh)

As I have said, Mr Derrick Amory had taken an interest in us almost from the beginning. He began the custom of inviting us each year to play at his home, Chevithorne Barton. He would have a few house guests and some local friends to dinner and afterwards we would entertain them in his large lounge where there was a beautiful Steinway grand piano. Our pianist by this time was Marjorie Tucker who, some years later, married another of our members, Alan Smale, before moving away from Tiverton. Marjorie was thrilled to have the opportunity to play on such a wonderful instrument and eventually she was invited to go to the house and practice on it whenever she liked, subject, I suppose, to other household arrangements.

There were about 16 or so boys in the Orchestra at that time and Marjorie was the only girl. We would arrive a little early to prepare and when 'Mr Derrick', as he was generally known, and his guests had finished their meal they would come in and listen to us play for an hour or so. Sometimes I had a soloist – either one of the Orchestra or perhaps a young singer from the Signpost Club: I remember one called June Southcott, who was a policeman's daughter. Afterwards we would be taken into the next room where a splendid and generous array of food was always laid out for us and as you can imagine, the boys did full justice to it!

I am afraid the boys were not always little angels (any more than today's youngsters). I recall one visit when Mr Derrick had just returned from a visit to Canada, bringing with him some duty free cigarettes for his guests, with which he had filled a number of cigarette boxes dotted about the rooms. He called me aside just as we were packing up to go home to inform me that he had found them all empty!

I was horrified, but he was quite nice about it and did not want to make a big fuss. However, I demanded to see inside every boy's instrument case and, lo and behold, most of them contained a handful of the missing cigarettes. Red-faced, they sheepishly returned every single one and mumbled their apologies before hurrying out to the waiting bus.

Another time, when we were playing at the Sampford Peverell Methodist Church, the irate Minister asked me to reprimand two of my lads who were playing leap-frog over the tombstones! The same boys were asked to leave the orchestra after a series of such incidents, including swinging from the balcony of the Congregational Church. Their grandmother, a nice old lady who was bringing them up, came to beg me to have them back and I did, but they were always quite a handful!

We used to have good support from local Councillors and other prominent people – Alderman Carpenter was one of several; but one of our most loyal supporters was Mrs Pierce, a former Mayoress of Tiverton. She managed to attend just about every one of our concerts. One winter's evening we drove through a heavy snowstorm to Holcombe Rogus where I had arranged (through an uncle of mine, Mr Jim Palfrey, who farmed there) to give a concert at the local church. I did not see Mrs Pierce among the crowd, but was not surprised in view of the terrible weather. Just as we were about to start the door opened and a figure appeared in the doorway clad in a fur coat and warm hat, both covered thickly in snow. "Here I am, Ronnie!" she called out cheerfully, "You can start now!" and of course it was Mrs Pierce.

I would do my best not to let anyone down if I had promised a concert, but as I had no deputy conductor it sometimes meant that I had to turn up even when I was ill. At one concert held in a village church (I think it might have been Poughill) I had the flu and could feel my temperature rising, so was very relieved when it was over. We never charged for these concerts, but I did ask for light refreshments to be provided afterwards for the youngsters. Invariably this would be most generously given by the ladies of the church – and the lads used to look forward to their little treat. On this occasion I felt too ill to want anything for myself, so while they all trooped into the room where it was laid out I sat quietly in a corner of the church. After a short while two of the ladies came back in and, not seeing me there, stood talking nearby. Said one to the other, "I've never seen anything like it! One minute the table was full of food and the next it was all gone – every bit of it!" I stayed where I was and kept very quiet!

Perhaps the most unusual 'garden party' we were ever asked to do was at the home of a well-known local doctor, Dr George Nicholson, who was quite a colourful character. Naturally, we assumed we would be entertaining some of his guests. However, when we all arrived in our good clothes and with our instruments he led us outside to his rather untidy garden where he handed out a selection of spades, forks and other tools, and exclaimed, cheerfully, "Now, lads! See if you can tidy this lot up for me before you have your tea!" We were dumbfounded, but set to work anyway, leaving the garden a lot tidier before we were taken inside to clean up. I have to say that we were given an excellent tea for our troubles.

On another occasion we were invited to Rackenford Manor, which was then home to Lord and Lady Eldon, this time to a genuine Garden Party. We were to play on the lawn in front of the large bay window of the lounge where there was a grand piano. The arrangement was that the piano would be moved to the window, which would be wide open, and Marjorie Tucker would be able to accompany us from there. I took several of our larger boys in with me to help move the piano to a suitable spot, but as we did so there was an ominous cracking noise and one leg of the instrument disappeared through the floorboards. I went to tell Lady Eldon what had happened. She and Lord Eldon came to inspect the damage. However, they did not seem in the least bit upset, or did not show it. Lady Eldon merely remarked that she was glad to know where the strange smell of rot had been coming from and now they could get it attended to. With some difficulty the piano, quite unharmed, was eased back up and we managed to find a safer part of the floor for it to stand.

Celebrity Concert: Alfredo Campoli

Holding a violin is like holding a young bird. It is vibrating under your touch and you must hold it without squeezing it. It is a good thing to cultivate the feeling of those sympathetic vibrations in dealing with people

(Yehudi Menuhin)

I had invited Angel Grande to come to Tiverton because I felt it important that the orchestra members should have the opportunity to hear some of the great musicians of our time. In Oxford I had been able to attend many good concerts and had learned a great deal from them, but in a small town like Tiverton there was no way of providing the same advantage unless I did something about it myself. And so, after the great success of my first Celebrity Concert, I began to plan another.

I had heard Alfredo Campoli on the radio many times and greatly admired his musicianship. I wrote, care of the BBC, and asked him if he would come to Tiverton. He replied that he would be happy to do so if he had other engagements in the South West and that he would contact me again if he were coming this way. I heard nothing for a time, but then he wrote and said he would be giving a recital in the Exeter Guildhall in October 1951 and if I could arrange a concert immediately after this, he would be happy to play for us. I quickly began to make all the necessary arrangements and the date was fixed. He invited me to attend the rehearsal for the Exeter concert and Chris Martin and I went there to meet the great man, who was very friendly and approachable. He was to play the Mendelssohn Violin concerto in E Minor with the Exeter Philharmonic Orchestra, conducted by Haig Marshall. At one point in the rehearsal he was plainly dissatisfied with the way the orchestra was performing, and, taking the baton from Haig Marshall's hand, began to conduct part of it himself.

After the rehearsal he took us both to the Clarendon Hotel, where he was staying, and gave us a very good lunch. I remember that he chose lobster and I was fascinated, as I had never seen one eaten before. I decided it was not for me, however. It looked far too complicated!

Our concert was on October 31st 1951 and once again we filled the Heathcoat Hall with a reported audience of 480, including many local dignitaries, and of course Mr Derrick Amory who now sent a regular donation towards our expenses. Among the pieces Campoli played for us were Saint-Saens' *Rondo Cappriccioso*, Air on the G-string (Bach) and some Kreisler variations, all of which had the audience completely spellbound.

PROGRAMME . . . . . PRICE SIXPENCE

TIVERTON YOUTH ORCHESTRA

President: Mr. D. H. Amory

CONDUCTOR: RONALD DAVEY

LEADER: DENIS GUNTER

150TH CONCERT

SOLO VIOLIN

CAMPOLI

ACCOMPANIST: FLORA KENT

THE HEATHCOAT HALL, TIVERTON

ON WEDNESDAY, OCTOBER 31st, 1951

At 7.30 p.m.

The orchestra played a selection of items and there were solos from Keith Green, a young boy soprano who also played violin and had recently joined us, and Marjorie Tucker who played Chopin's *Fantasia Impromptu*. Mr Campoli's violin was a 'Rocca', which was sold in 1999 for £128,000 – and I had been allowed to play on it during his visit! When he heard that I often provided spare strings to the young players out of my own pocket he sent a large box of his own used ones. He always changed all his strings before a concert whether or not this was strictly necessary, so they were all practically new. I handed them out to the members and used some myself for many years. I know of one founder member who tells me he still has some. As with Angel Grande, I had arranged rooms at the Bridge Guest House for him and his accompanist, Miss Daphne Ibbot, and they seemed pleased to welcome such distinguished guests.

Meanwhile, we continued to play as before, giving concerts in and around the district and with the Signpost Club and Tiverton Dramatic Society. By this time several new members had joined us, including a young pianist, Eileen Randoll. At first she would stand at the piano with Marjorie, turning the pages and sometimes played some of the easier pieces, while learning from Marjorie some of the skills needed to accompany an orchestra. She became more proficient and confident with practice, of course, and some years later returned to become our regular accompanist.

This picture was taken not long before I met Margaret — ca. 1951

It was while playing for the Tiverton Dramatic Society's production of *The Happiest Days of Your Life* in the New Hall one week in the winter of 1951 that I first met my future wife, Margaret (née Robinson), who was taking part. It was the final dress rehearsal and the hall was extremely chilly. In between scenes I could see her shivering, so I put my coat around her shoulders. We began chatting and the rest, as they say, is history. She soon became involved in my work with the Youth Orchestra and attended nearly all our concerts from then on. She was living with her aunt and uncle at Post Hill at the time and I had arranged to pick her up at the corner of Mayfair for one concert. It was snowing heavily and in my haste to get there in good time I completely forgot about her. She stood for nearly an hour before I remembered. Surprisingly, she still agreed to marry me when I later proposed!

One play the Dramatic Society performed around that time was a light comedy, *Queen Elizabeth Slept Here*. In the audience was someone from the Tone Dale Psychiatric Hospital, which has since closed. He felt it would be ideal to entertain the patients, having nothing unsuitable in its content and had an easy plot to follow. They asked if the orchestra would go as well, to make up the programme with incidental music. Margaret was not in the original cast, taking her turn at one of the backstage jobs, but several of the members were unavailable that day and substitutes had to be made so she agreed to stand in as the maid.

It was quite an undertaking for the backstage crew to transport all the scenery and props and set them up, so once I had set up our stands and laid out the music there was quite a while when we had nothing to do. A man in a white coat came up and asked us if we would like to look around the kitchens where he said he worked. Assuming he was a member of the catering staff, I agreed and went off with about a dozen of my orchestra lads, all trooping behind our guide. We were shown the huge kitchen area with vast arrays of equipment – it was a very large hospital with a great many patients – and it was all quite imposing. Then he opened the door of an enormous meat refrigerator with all the stores hanging up inside on great hooks. He invited us to take a closer look but once we were all inside he quickly stepped back out and closed the door.

So there we were, standing in the dark and cold, wondering what on earth was going on! Some of the boys began to be rather frightened and I did my best to reassure them, though to be honest, I was quite alarmed myself. We seemed to be in there for ages and it was pretty chilly. I felt around for something to press for help, but couldn't find anything, or any way to open the door from the inside.

Just as we were all getting really worried, the door suddenly opened and we all hurried out, but there was nobody in sight. Then one of the staff we had met in the concert hall came along. He said everyone was waiting to begin and they had been wondering where we all were. I explained what had happened and he asked me to try to point out the person who had shown us round. He turned out to be a patient who was allowed to work in the kitchens sometimes! "You were lucky he came back," I was told, "We might not have thought of looking in there for you and it would not normally have been opened again until tomorrow morning." So we had a fortunate escape!

The entertainment went off without further hitch, except for one or two of the audience behaving rather oddly, but we had expected that. One young man kept running down the centre aisle, tapping me on the shoulder and then running back again as I conducted. It was a bit disconcerting, but I managed to ignore it. On the whole, though, the event went very well.

One big event I recall in the early 1950s was the Gilbert and Sullivan Anniversary Week – a series of concerts held in the former Electric Theatre (now a bingo hall). From a press cutting of the event it is recorded that we played each evening before the screening of a film on the lives of the two composers.

Those who played included; Basil Pearce, Bob Grabham, Marjorie Tucker, Eileen Randoll, Keith Green, David Walker, Ronald Sharland, Alan Smale, Michael Chidgey, Edgar Smith, Keith Butt, Mervyn Garland, 'Nanto' Williams, John Skinner, Peter Squires, Maurice Davey, Irvine Bendelow, Patrick Rudell, Michael Dummett, Raymond Davey, Brian Haskins, Philip Williams, Martin Troake, Trevor Chilcott and Gerald Burton.

In April 1953 Margaret and I were married at the Methodist Church. Chris Martin was my Best Man – and we felt we had to involve the orchestra members in our most special day. They formed an archway of violins for us as we emerged from the church, and later, at the reception in the Heathcoat Hall, they sat on the stage and played background music for us. Young Keith Green sang a few solos, and after the reception there was a good array of refreshments for them One member, Irvine Bendelow, on behalf of the orchestra, presented me with a handsome barometer, suitably inscribed, which is of course still a treasured possession.

Those who were mentioned in the report of the Gilbert and Sullivan event were approximately the same as those who attended our wedding – a day to remember.

Celebrity Concert: Tom Jenkins

And the night shall be filled with music
and the cares that infest the day,
Shall fold their tents like the Arabs
and as silently steal away.

(Longfellow)

I had begun to plan my next Celebrity Concert soon after Campoli's and had written to another well-known violinist, Tom Jenkins, who used to be heard regularly on a radio programme called *Palm Court Hotel* with the Palm Court Orchestra. It was a fictitious setting for an entertainment based on the type of orchestra often found playing at smart hotels at that time and would feature light music and some excellent soloists. When Albert Sandler (the original regular soloist) became ill, Tom Jenkins had taken over and was very popular. As with Campoli, I was told that I would have to wait for a suitable slot in his busy schedule. Eventually, on March 12th 1954, he came to Tiverton with his wife Michelle whom he had recently married, and his accompanist Gerald Gover, himself a noted musician. Because they knew the proprietors of the Hartnoll Hotel at the time, Mr and Mrs Sinton, they made their own arrangements and stayed there. There was some anxiety on the day, as they did not arrive as early as they had promised – but finally they turned up at our small terraced home in John Street where Margaret, who was shortly expecting our first child, had prepared a Devonshire cream tea for them. She had made all kinds of scones, cakes, trifles etc, and Mr Gover's eyes lit up at the spread, but Mr Jenkins declined, saying he never ate much before a concert. However, he accepted a cup of tea while Gerald Gover and Mrs Jenkins sat down and enjoyed our hospitality.

My late father, Bill Davey, had a hobby at that time of growing and curing his own tobacco for his pipe. He enthusiastically demonstrated this for Mr Gover, who later inscribed in my autograph book, "Thanks for the paternal tobacco!" as he had been given a sample to try!

I then took them to the Heathcoat Hall to show Mr Jenkins where he would be playing. The theme tune of the radio series was a piece called *Roses from the South*. I had bought it especially for the concert and we had been rehearsing it for several weeks. When he saw it on one of the music stands he groaned, "Oh no – please don't play that one – I'm really tired of hearing it wherever I go!" So I had to remove all the copies and replace them quickly with another piece that the players already knew.

Once again the hall was packed to capacity and our visitors were warmly welcomed by the Mayor and Mayoress, Cllr and Mrs Harold Shapland. Also present were Lady Amory and Mr Derrick Amory, who still supported us as often as his busy life as Tiverton's MP would allow.

For each half of the concert the Tiverton Youth Orchestra played a few pieces – and then Tom Jenkins took the stage. After the interval I resumed my place at the conductor's stand, glanced at the orchestra and was amazed to see him sitting among the second violins where he played alongside them until it was time for his second appearance. Mr Jenkins was, however, in very poor health and sadly, only a few years later, in 1957, I heard that he had died. More recently his widow Michelle commissioned a book on his life, a copy of which I have, together with a charming letter from her, saying how well she remembered their visit to Tiverton. His Stradivari violin, which he had bought in 1948 for £1,250 was sold in 1995 to a ten-year-old German girl for £340,000.

In 1955 my employer, Mr Dart, died and I decided to start my own business. After a short time at Rackenford I took over premises at Riverside, Gold Street, carrying out motor body repairs. I was there until I retired in 1976.

In January 1957 we were rehearsing as usual at the Heathcoat School in King Street, ready for a pantomime when a man walked in and introduced himself as John Irvine from the BBC radio programme *Down Your Way*. They used to visit a different town each week and talk to various local people. He interrupted our rehearsal to chat to me about the Youth Orchestra and also to some of the members. I later heard that he had been to see others in the town, including Mr Brian Elsworthy, a leading member of the Tiverton Dramatic Society. It was he who kindly gave me a copy of the recording later, as he owned a tape recorder – not many people had one at the time. I later received a letter of thanks and a cheque for ten guineas from the BBC for our funds.

Now that I had a wife and a young daughter as well as caring for my elderly father and managing my firm, I found that I had less time to devote to other activities. Many of the older boys of the orchestra also had other interests and so, at this time, I decided not to hold regular rehearsals any more, or take on so many engagements.

Instead, whenever there was a Signpost Club production, or a Dramatic Society play, I would contact a group of ex-members and a few other local musicians and we would perform under the name of the Tiverton Youth Orchestra. This continued for a long time, until eventually both of these organisations made other arrangements for their musical requirements and we were no longer needed, Even after this, however, I would occasionally gather together a group of musicians to play at certain events in the town.

I still had a few violin pupils – I remember one used to keep his fish and chip supper warm in his violin case on his way home and the violin always smelled of them!

The Orchestra has a Fresh Start

If everybody insisted on playing first violin, we would have no orchestras. Respect every musician in his own field.

(From *Advice to Young Musicians,* Robert Schumann 1848)

In the early 1960s, two families had moved to Tiverton and were making an impact in the field of education, especially where music was concerned. Roy and Maureen Rendell and Wilf and Berice Saunders each had a young family and were concerned at the lack of musical opportunity in the town at that time. Wilf and Maureen, both Junior School teachers, set out to do something about the situation. Encouraged by the Music Department of the Devon Education Office, under Mr Andrew Mowll and Mr Brian Ley, they began to arrange a series of Saturday morning 'workshops' using the former Grammar School premises as a centre, where the Castle School is now.

I had already met Wilf who had begun to teach violin to a small group of children, including his young daughter, Heather. He had been told of my involvement in the Tiverton Youth Orchestra, and one day he came to ask if I would be willing to go along and take a group of young strings players. Each instrument section rehearsed separately and according to ability. As they made progress they were brought together to learn how to play as an orchestra, which is quite another skill in itself. I was not sure if I actually wanted to get too involved in all this, but I went along to see what it was like and found myself really enjoying these sessions. My chief interest was the strings section and after a while I agreed to get them all together for extra practices. To save hiring a hall, Maureen offered us the use of a large 'barn' that was part of her home at New Place, which she and Roy had recently purchased. It was a bit draughty, but we met there each week for some time, using much of the music I had kept from my earlier days – and we all gained a lot from the experience. I remember Maureen used to supply the hot drinks to keep us going!

At one time or another, all the Rendell children, Andrew, Anne and John and all the Saunders children, Trevor, David, Heather and Richard eventually played as members.

One day in 1970 I met Viscount Amory, who had been granted this title on completion of his term of office as Chancellor of the Exchequer in 1960 and so was no longer 'Mr Derrick' – though as friendly and interested as ever. I told him a little about these Saturday morning workshops and our extra practices at New Place. He asked if I would consider re-forming the Tiverton Youth Orchestra as a regular commitment, using this nucleus of new, young players. I went home and discussed the idea with Margaret but resisted the idea for some time as I felt it might take up far too much time and energy. However, I was being persuaded on all sides – Lord Amory, Wilf and Maureen, Brian Ley – and began to think it might be a good idea. Most importantly to me, Margaret promised to support me if I chose to do it. I knew I would have to rely on her cooperation for such an undertaking.

So one evening in 1970, having placed a letter in the local press, inviting anyone who was interested to come along, I turned up at the Grammar School hall and set out a few chairs and music stands, wondering if anyone would bother to turn up. To my surprise, quite a large number of keen young people began to assemble, with a varied range of instruments, and I found I had not enough copies of my music to go round. There had seldom been more than about 20 players in the original orchestra and here I was, faced with more than double this number!

My son John, at the age of 12, decided he would like to learn percussion, having tried violin and piano without much enthusiasm. He went on a course organised by the Devon County Education Music Department and was very fortunate to be taught by no less a person than James Blades, one of the best percussionists of the day.

When I tried to track down the drums I had once had, but lent to a former member, nobody seemed to know what had happened to them. I wanted a set for John to play, as he and a friend were ready to make up our percussion section. Lord Amory came to our rescue with a generous donation to buy a good second-hand set – and asked to be kept informed of any other requirements.

A group of TYO members ready for a rehearsal at Tiverton Grammar School — 18th January 1972

The staff of the Education Music Department were always very keen to offer assistance and advice without being intrusive.

A young girl, Christine Bolton, offered to play the piano for us and we found her to be a versatile and accomplished musician. I noticed, sitting among the string players, several familiar faces, including Trevor Chilcott, who had been a founder member and, seeing my letter, had decided to come back. I also noticed another gentleman who would not mind me saying that he was not exactly a 'youth'. This was Mr Reg Tayler, who had moved to Tiverton from Chesterfield and wanted to be able to play his violin again. It is true I had not specified an exact age limit – so he remained with us, only retiring when he reached his 80th birthday some years later. For a long time he was our official Chairman, a post later taken over by Trevor.

We had regular rehearsals from then on, although we later moved to the Secondary School (now Tiverton High School) for a time, as the music teacher of the Grammar School greatly disapproved of us. I never discovered exactly why. When I tried to meet him to clear the air over anything he might feel concerned about, he simply declined. We had a few problems over the years with a small number of people who seemed bent on spoiling things for us, but on the whole I found overwhelming good will and co-operation. Looking back, I think it might have been that I was not controlled or bound by the constraints of any official body, which irritated a few people. When, some years later, Mr Derek Stone gave his rendering of Frank Sinatra's song, *My Way*, at one of our concerts, I felt it rather apt to my style of doing things!

I did my best to make the rehearsals fun, with an informal atmosphere, and talked, as I have always done, to everyone at an equal level, from the youngest upwards. This was, after all, meant to be a leisure activity, so I tried not to let it seem like an extension of their school lessons. I think I generally succeeded in this. That is not to say I didn't sometimes yell at them, either to be quiet or to do as I asked when getting them to play a piece the way I wanted it done. There will also be members who can recall being tapped on the head with my baton from time to time! We drew our members mainly from schools of course, over quite a wide area – and there was a good, friendly relationship among most of them. Our choice of music was also quite varied, mainly light classical pieces and I managed to introduce them to a wide range of composers, some of whom they would otherwise probably never have come to know.

As people became aware that we were now meeting again on a regular basis we received several donations of unwanted instruments and a huge box of stands. We soon had a pool of equipment, which, together with some violins of my own, we loaned out to members for a modest charge. This covered insurance and occasional repairs. They would sign an undertaking to keep them safe and in good order. We had only a few major mishaps – a foot through a cello left on the floor; the neck snapped off another when it was being carried through a swing door; a trumpet which was sat upon and squashed somewhat – but all were genuine accidents and the owners suitably mortified. I never minded if the borrowed instruments were used for musical events other than our own; for example, several asked if they could play at school concerts.

However, it was another matter when members were using school instruments. There was one memorable occasion when we had a big concert and I had a frantic phone call the day before from two Grammar School girls who played French Horns. The instruments were locked away and the girls had been refused permission to take them home and use them at the concert. I contacted Lord Amory for advice and, without hesitation he told me to go to Exeter and buy two Horns and send him the bill, which I did. I felt not so much angry as rather sad that anyone could be quite so petty, as we could have worked together for our mutual benefit and that of the children concerned. Incidentally, a few years earlier, before I had any thought of resuming the Orchestra, I had donated several good violins to the same school! But that's life.

Our ties with Blundell's School strengthened about this time, encouraged by Lord Amory who was, I believe, a School governor. Mr Keith Abrahams and his successor, Mr Paul Matthews, were Heads of the Music Department and ready to forge links with us. The school's policy was changing and boys were being encouraged to take some part in the life of the town. I enquired if any of their school orchestra or brass band would like to come and join us at rehearsals, and they were happy to allow this, subject of course to other commitments. For some years I had a regular selection of their pupils taking part and even one or two teachers. I felt that there were benefits on both sides, though a few hearts were broken when romances blossomed between their boys and some of our girls. I am pleased to say that, without exception, successive headmasters at Blundell's School have been most helpful.

Less than a year after we reformed, our young pianist's family moved away from the area. I remembered Eileen Randoll, now Mrs Pengelly, who had been with us before – and she readily agreed to come back, and remained as our pianist for some years.

There's More to Being a Conductor Than you Might Think!

I never used a score when conducting my orchestra. Does a lion-tamer enter a cage with a book on how to tame a lion?

(Dimitri Mitropoulos)

I never did have a properly elected Committee as such, but in the early years Maureen Rendell acted as our Treasurer and Margaret did most of the secretarial work. We had parents' meetings from time to time, mostly regarding fund-raising – and early on we met to decide on what the youngsters should wear at concerts. The general opinion was that white shirts or blouses, with black or dark grey trousers for the boys and men, and long black skirts for the girls were the simplest for parents to obtain and would look neat. A few of the girls were a bit rebellious at not being allowed to choose what they wore, but I could not be sure they would go for suitable alternatives. My doubts were confirmed when one young lady (and a local church minister's daughter at that) defiantly turned up in her version of our dress code. Her blouse was certainly white, but completely transparent – and her skirt was, it is true, long and black, but with a slit up one side, right to the top of her leg! As she was seated right at the front of the stage, I rather suspect that a few members of the audience were not entirely absorbed in the music, that evening!

Another mother complained at my insistence on long skirts, on the grounds that her two daughters were quite young and she felt short ones would do. However, one of them was a little on the plump side and also her chair was right at the front of the platform. I asked Margaret to explain, as tactfully as she could, that skirts ride up when girls are seated, giving the front row of the audience quite an eyeful! I think she saw our point of view.

Quite apart from the musical side, I often found myself in the position of adviser and comforter to some of the young people. Perhaps there was a problem at home – a split in the family, or a bereavement, or bullying at school. There was often a hazard at being seen to carry an instrument case and boys especially had to go to great lengths to avoid being picked on, carrying them in sports bags or hiding them in lockers. They would come to me with their worries and of course I did my best to help when I could.

The scope of the orchestra used to vary a good deal from year to year. Older members, many of whom had become excellent players and a great asset, would leave to go on to colleges or universities or to take jobs elsewhere, while some developed other interests and simply left – it happens in any organisation. In their places came new, younger players who needed time to gain experience in playing with us, so sometimes we had to go back to simpler pieces for a while, or choose easy arrangements. I spent many hours re-writing and arranging pieces to suit our newer members, so they would not be frightened off by music that was too difficult for them. From time to time, I found I had no one at all playing certain instruments, or, as happened more than once, over 20 beginners, all playing the clarinet!

At other times I had a good assortment of more advanced players and we could again tackle something a bit more challenging. For a time our brass section was very strong as we had a number of young players from the Town Band who had joined us. I found a lively piece called *Latin Americana*, a selection of rhythmic dance melodies, which went down very well with everyone, players and audience alike, and was very different from our normal light classical repertoire. At one concert, all the brass and percussion sections donned huge Mexican sombreros for this, which was quite a novelty, especially when they all stood, like the 'Big Bands' did, for the highlights.

Alfredo Campoli Returns to Tiverton

Talent instantly recognises genius

Sir Arthur Conan Doyle

Once we had settled down and begun to build up a nice little repertoire of pieces I decided to try to arrange another visit from Alfredo Campoli. He readily agreed to come as soon as his plans permitted. The first thing he said in his letter, however, was, "Make sure the piano is properly tuned this time!" This referred to his first visit, when I had arranged to have the Heathcoat Hall piano specially tuned by Moon's of Exeter, which was the main music shop there at the time. They sent up their tuner, a blind person, to carry out the work. It sounded fine to me, but when Mr Campoli went down to the hall before the concert to check everything, he compared it with his own 'A' and found it was a whole tone out. He looked at me in despair and said, "You *******! You promised you'd have it tuned perfectly!" I had to send for the tuner to return immediately, who apologised and re-tuned it to Mr.Campoli's satisfaction. Anxious to avoid such a situation again, I went to see Mr Annett of Beeston's, a long-established music shop in Bampton Street, and he agreed to come and see to the piano at the Secondary School personally. I am glad to say there was no problem on this second occasion.

So, in 1972, for the second time, Tiverton people were able to enjoy hearing this great musician. He had semi-retired by now and asked to have a room at The Hartnoll Hotel which was not too far from the School Hall.

Once again the concert was a sell-out, with Lord Amory sitting as usual in his special armchair in the front row. This time I had Margaret to help with the arrangements, which made things easier for me. She had sent out invitations with complimentary tickets to people such as the Mayor and Lord Amory. As she conducted Lord Amory to his seat, he remarked that he had not yet paid for his ticket. On being told that his was complimentary, he replied, "Nonsense, you can't afford to do that sort of thing. Now, how much is it?" Rather embarrassed, Margaret told him and he proffered some money, which was about 20 pence too much. "Mind

Concert at Tiverton School (now Tiverton High School) — 1972
Felicity Gibling, Jacki Attwood, Alfredo Campoli, Teresa Lockyer, Heather Saunders

you bring back the change," he instructed, which of course she did, marvelling that he had only recently handed over a couple of hundred pounds for the two French Horns without batting an eyelid!

Mr Campoli was wonderful with the young people, having his photograph taken with a few and chatting to them all. He enthralled the whole audience, proving that he was still on top form. However, he was too tired afterwards to stay and sign the many programmes being waved at him, so we collected them all up and later took them to the Hotel. Together with our son John, we sat and had coffee with him after his meal and watched him as he signed the huge pile. He had some words of wisdom for John, who was then 14. "The secret of success in anything is self-discipline," he told John, "If you can't control yourself, you will never be able to control anything else." Wise words indeed, and never forgotten.

Soon after the second Campoli concert several of our members were auditioned and allowed to join the Devon Youth Orchestra. This is drawn from young players all over the County and it is quite an honour to be selected. I don't know if it is the same now, but back then they would meet together once or twice a year for a residential weekend or sometimes longer, which would end in a concert for parents and others to attend. One year the Devon Arts Society commissioned a special work – *The Red Sea* – from Malcolm Williamson, and on this occasion a wider ranger of pupils were invited to take part, not only musicians but singers. John was among those chosen and he joined the percussion section. They all spent a week at Dartington Hall. Malcolm Williamson himself turned up to oversee the final rehearsal, and the final production was a great success.

Through Margaret's involvement with the Brownies and the local Guides, we took part during the 1970s in a series of large Christmas concerts held at Blundell's School and organised by the Rotary Club. We had tiered staging on the platform, with the Youth Orchestra arranged in front below. Over a hundred Scouts, Cubs, Guides and Brownies from all over the District took part. The audience comprised pensioners, brought in by buses and cars – and after a strenuous afternoon of communal carol singing they were given a good tea, including the obligatory mince pies, before being transported home. It was hard work, but always good fun for everyone.

Garden Parties at Brewin Road

You have Van Gogh's ear for music

(Billy Wilder)

At the end of 1973 Margaret and I were appointed as resident Wardens at the flats in Brewin Road, where we were to remain for nearly 14 years. Part of our job was to encourage an active social life for the tenants, but there was little money in the kitty by the time we arrived, the last of it having been spent on a Christmas dinner. I thought we might arrange a garden party in the summer, with the Youth Orchestra taking part, to raise some funds for treats. Everyone was very excited about the idea, as they had never done anything quite like it before. We roped in anyone willing to help and there were many offers. Home helps agreed to serve refreshments, and other people in the street offered to run sideshows, skittles, etc. Some of the tenants' families enthusiastically joined in, and a handful of Margaret's Brownies turned up. Our daughter Jeanne organised a tombola stall with a prize every time, while the tenants themselves had been busy making cakes, knitting tea-cosies and various other articles, as well as hunting out bric-a-brac and groceries for the stalls.

The Youth Orchestra turned out in force and played all afternoon in return for a steady supply of cold drinks, as it was a very hot day. It seemed as if all West Exe had turned up to support us. Everyone thoroughly enjoyed the event and we made enough money for a free trip to the coast, with enough left over towards the next Christmas dinner. It was quite an occasion for the street and I wondered what they thought of our music, because not many would have been likely to come to our concerts. I asked a small girl what she thought of it. "Well, it was all right," she said, "and I liked the music. But *you* didn't do much, did you? You just stood there and waved that stick about all the time!"

From then on, the Garden Party became an annual event, but instead of the Youth Orchestra, the Town Band played for them for a good many years, which was much appreciated. I am glad to see that Garden Parties are still a feature of the flats' social life to this day.

The Start of Our Twinning Activities

Music knows no boundaries

(Klaus Giesen)

In September 1975 I was invited to go to Chinon with a party from the town's Twinning Association. I had thought about taking the orchestra there, but could see no way of arranging this – twinning was not making much progress at that time. After an enthusiastic start through some school contacts and other exchanges arranged by Cllr Mrs Margaret (Peggy) Allen it had fizzled out somewhat. This new delegation was intended to try to improve things and was made up as follows: Cllr and Mrs Frank Suter (a local solicitor) Cllr and Mrs Eric Shapland, Mr Norman Holbrook (the headmaster of Heathcoat Junior School), Mrs Elizabeth Cunningham (of Social Services), Mr Brian Reade, (a teacher of French at the Grammar School) and myself. We went by ferry, driving in two cars, and stayed in the annex of a small hotel in Chinon for a long weekend.

A programme of engagements had been planned for us and we were all made most welcome. Also in Chinon that weekend were some officials from Hofheim, a town near Frankfurt in West Germany. They were also twinned with Chinon and had with them their Akkordeon Orchester, which at that time was composed of about 30 young players together with their teachers and organisers. Arrangements had been made for us to sit in on a council meeting at the Town Hall, which was of course particularly interesting to our two local councillors. They were keen to see how things were conducted in another country. As you probably know, one is not permitted to speak at such a meeting unless authorised. However, I was so anxious to get permission to bring the Youth Orchestra to Chinon that I am afraid I broke all the rules by standing up and telling them a bit about us. Poor Eric Shapland was very embarrassed and kept tugging at my jacket in an effort to get me to sit down and be quiet – but their Mayor, Monsieur Daydé, signalled that I should be allowed to continue. At the end everyone applauded and I was promised that a date for a visit would be arranged.

Another event we attended was a big ceremony in the wine caves, when the Wine Producers' Society wore their splendid scarlet robes, and various honours were bestowed on members. Mr Suter was to be made an honorary member and part of the ceremony involved him being expected to drink a huge glass of the famous red local wine in one go – a task he found quite difficult but valiantly accomplished, much to everyone's delight! I remember being introduced to a very attractive French actress who I believe was very well known at the time, but I am afraid I cannot recall her name. During my visit I was able to hear the Akkordeon Orchester play – and they really were most impressive. One of their members, a young man called Hans-Jürgen Mock could speak quite good English and he introduced me to their Chairman, Herr Günter Powils, and also to some of their town officials including the Mayor. I explained about my proposed visit to Chinon with the Youth Orchestra and one of them (I believe it was Herr Flaccus) said, jovially, "Well, you must also come to Hofheim!" Perhaps I should mention that the excellent French wine had flowed very freely that weekend and before any of us quite knew it, we had agreed that a visit to Hofheim could, and indeed would, be arranged.

Talking to Hans-Jürgen Mock during our first contact with Hofheim in Chinon — 1974

During the proceedings the French people stood up and sang a rousing traditional song in praise of their wine – and the Germans had responded with one of theirs, so we felt we ought to uphold the honour of our own country with a suitable rendition. We could not think what we could do until I suddenly remembered *Widdecombe Fair*.

While the others gathered together and hastily jotted down what they could remember of the words, I enquired if anyone had a violin I might borrow, on which to accompany them. Someone was sent off, returning with a genuine Stradivari, which had miraculously been borrowed either from the Museum or some local personage. The man who brought it insisted on standing next to me the whole time and as soon as we finished it was swiftly removed and taken back from whence it came. I have to say that we managed quite a creditable rendering of our Devon folk song, which went down very well with the other guests.

On our return to Tiverton I called a meeting of members and parents to ask if anyone would like to go to Chinon. Nearly all of them seemed keen, so we fixed a date during a school half term break. Brian Reade kindly offered to steer us through all the necessary formalities and the correspondence between the Chinon Twinning Committee and ourselves. He had organised several school exchanges and of course spoke French fluently, so his assistance was invaluable. We were total novices at this sort of thing. The Chinon Twinning committee agreed the date and promised to arrange host families for us all. We chose a programme of suitable music, practiced hard, and held a series of fund-raising events to help subsidise the cost of the trip. This included a 'play-in' at the Town Hall by kind permission of the Mayor, which lasted seven and a half hours, with 62 pieces played in all. By now we had a few other adults, including one or two Town Band members.

Eventually the day came when we set out on the long coach journey to the ferry and then down through France. Once we were across the Channel and well on our way, Brian phoned ahead to let them know our estimated time of arrival. Then, at about 4 pm, we finally arrived outside the Town Hall where the Mayor, Monsieur Daydé, the Twinning Committee and a crowd of people stood ready to welcome us. Exhausted after our 20-hour journey, we stumbled off the coach and were ushered into a large room where we stood while the Mayor made a lengthy and, to most of us, totally incomprehensible speech. Then our names were read out in turn and a stream of smiling local families came forward to claim their guests. I sometimes wonder if I would be quite so carefree these days, in handing over quite young children – some were under 12 – into the hands of complete strangers, few of whom spoke any English!

In fact, I later discovered that very little had been done to find accommodation for us until just a couple of weeks beforehand, when an appeal had been placed in the local press asking for volunteers to turn up on the day. However, I don't think any of our people were unhappy with their hosts, even with the language barrier, though some didn't seem to realise quite how tired we all were. I know one young girl who stayed with a dairy farmer's family and had to go with them on the late milk round before going home to change, rest and have a meal. It had to be done and I suppose they were reluctant to leave a strange child alone in the house. A few had to face some rather exotic meals, such as fried sheep's brains, but on the whole, things went quite well.

Margaret and I, together with half a dozen adults in the group, were given rooms in an hotel belonging to Madame Perrault (one of the Twinning Committee) and her husband. We were treated very kindly. After a rest, shower and an excellent meal we all felt a bit more human, but the programme which they had planned for us included a concert in the Town Hall that very evening at 8pm!

We hurried off to set up all the stands, music etc, but were warned that Chinon was not really used to musical concerts, so we might not have a very big audience. We need not have worried, because long before it was due to start the hall began to fill up and people were seen hurrying off to seek out extra chairs from various parts of the building. Soon it was 'standing room only' and all the children in the audience had to be asked to come forward and sit on the floor at the front, so that adults could take their seats and the children would see more easily.

Our choice of music seemed to go down well, especially Mussorgski's *The Old Castle* from *Pictures at an Exhibition*, as Chinon is very proud of its ancient fortification which stands on a hill dominating the landscape. Brian Reade introduced our items and explained a little about the Tiverton Youth Orchestra – and that, as there was no government backing, we had held events to pay for our visit. Everyone seemed quite impressed.

In the interval between my earlier visit to Chinon and this one, the Tiverton Twinning Committee had decided to try to do something about the lack of a appropriate songs to represent our town at international gatherings – and had held a competition to compose a suitable 'Song for Tiverton'. The winning entry was written by the headmaster of Blundell's School, Mr Clive Gimpson. He allowed several of his pupils and a teacher (Alan Furse) to accompany us, including Stephen Mudge, who had an excellent baritone voice. He sang the new song for the first time since the competition. This went down very well, as did our other soloists, all Orchestra members, including Gordon Hills (trombone); Claire Taylor, then aged 13, who sang to her own guitar accompaniment; Teresa Foster who gave a piano solo; Bridget Budge with her violin; and Steven Russell on the trumpet. Our brass players were feeling very hot and dry and a large supply of Evian water was sent for, which was much needed and appreciated.

But by this time everyone was feeling extremely tired – and one young girl, Sue, burst into tears through sheer exhaustion and had to be taken home – yet still they wanted us to play on. I think it was about 11 pm before we finally put away our music.

We had a full programme of outings, including a guided walk around the town, with many historical features and a coach trip to see some of the famous and beautiful castles of the Loire Valley.

While we were being shown around Chinon Castle, another young member, Garry Randoll, who was studying French at the Grammar School, took over some of the interpreting as the local guide explained its history to us. In one room there were some tapestries depicting various historical scenes. We all stood facing them, with the exception of a certain teenage couple, who took the opportunity to cuddle up together on a large antique sofa, which stood at the back of the room. Unfortunately for them, there was another tapestry on the wall behind them and the tour guide finally invited us to view this one, which meant that we all turned at once to face the other way and were unwitting witnesses to this romantic moment! I remember exactly who they were, but will spare them the embarrassment of being named in this book.

During our visit we gave three other concerts, one being at a local old people's home where we sent a few of the younger girls round with a large tin of Roses chocolates, which went down very well. Another was in the

Town Hall again, but this time for the local Junior School pupils. The other concert was in the Lycée Rabelais, their High School, where the school exchanges had first begun. At this one we were entertained in return by a small group of young guitar players. The Mayor, Monsieur Daydé, took the time to attend every one of our concerts, and after the last we were given what we were assured was a typical school meal. This made a great impression on our young people as it was excellent, starting with pâté and toast and ending with fresh fruit. I forget the main course, but it was certainly of a high standard. Monsieur Daydé was very taken with young Claire Taylor, who had played her guitar and sung at each concert, and he insisted on giving her a hug and a kiss, which resulted in a certain amount of teasing from the rest of the members afterwards.

The concert for the younger children was quite an experience. They had evidently never been to a musical concert before and had no idea of how they were to respond. They behaved very well and seemed to enjoy the programme, especially Gordon Hills' performance of his popular trombone solo, *The Acrobat*, which is very amusing with a lot of sliding notes. Evidently they had been told that when the music stopped they were to clap, but they were a little too enthusiastic about obeying this instruction. Every time we came to a pause, even of only a couple of bars' rest, they decided the piece was over and began to clap. The orchestra found this rather distracting and so before long I found myself trying to avoid any pauses which might be long enough to give them a chance to applaud again before the end of the piece. We finished the programme well ahead of time!

Before the concert began, and during the short interval, the children were very interested in the various instruments and gathered round asking questions and wanting to try them. Garry came to my rescue and interpreted for us. I think they learned a lot from our concert and hope it had some lasting effect on their attitude to music.

When our time came to go home we were all sorry to leave our kind friends who had made us all so welcome. As we began to load up our things on to the bus in the town square, ready to set off for home, quite a number of people came up to shake our hands and say goodbye. A few handed us packets of cakes and biscuits to share on the journey home.

Unfortunately they had no similar organisation for us to invite back to Tiverton, and we never made a return visit. It was a tremendous help for us to have had Brian Reade with us for this, our first visit abroad. To have done so without speaking the language or knowing about various formalities would have been very daunting and I was very grateful for all that he did to help us.

You might think that was enough excitement to last a while, but not so. Immediately on my return I tried to make contact with the Russian Embassy with a view to taking the orchestra there. You must remember that this was in the days of the so-called 'Cold War' and such contacts were hard to achieve, even though the atmosphere between our two countries had certainly improved more recently. They seemed to have no means of dealing with an 'unofficial' organisation like ours. I did receive some application forms back, but they were very complex and seemed to want to know absolutely everything about every member, virtually down to their second cousin twice removed and their granny's shoe size. So I decided it was all going to be too much red tape for me!

I then heard about a Norwegian Youth Orchestra in Stavanger, where Tiverton Grammar School had also made an exchange and their conductor, a Mr Oliver, was keen to consider the idea of exchanging visits with us. We had quite a lengthy correspondence and he sounded a really nice person. However, he could not persuade the parents of his members to allow their children to stay with families. They would only consider a Youth Hostel arrangement in each place. As this was not what I really wanted and there was, in any case, no suitable premises at this end, the whole plan fell through. Perhaps it was just as well. I found that it would have been a very expensive visit for us to make, as the cost of living in Norway was very high and the monetary exchange rate very low.

Elizabeth Hunt

A Celebrity from 'Down Under'

The reward of a thing well done,
is to have done it

(Ralph Waldo Emerson)

I moved on to my next project, which was to be another Celebrity concert. I have always kept in touch with my friend, Christopher Martin. By this time he had played with several excellent orchestras on the continent and he had met and married a talented Australian cellist, Annette Rosefield. They had come to England to give a concert with Peter Clack, a professional French Horn player and an old friend of Christopher's. I asked him if he could recommend someone who might be willing to come and play for us. He suggested a gifted young violinist, Elizabeth Hunt, who would be coming to England for a series of engagements. She readily agreed, but I was asked to make all the arrangements through her agent, Miss Barbara Graham.

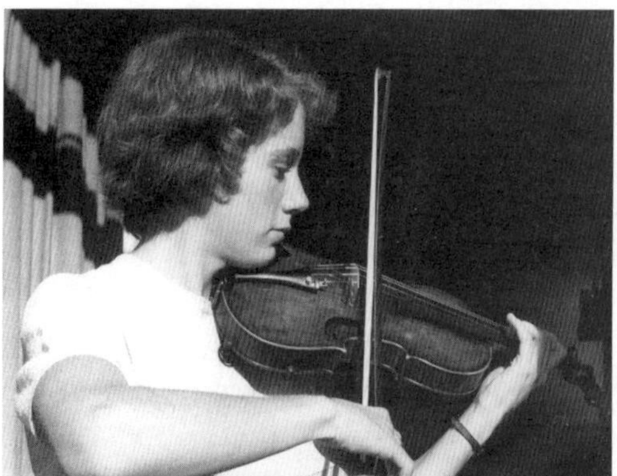

Elizabeth Hunt

As the date drew closer I had to telephone her a few times concerning various details, and she wanted to know about our Orchestra. As we chatted I mentioned that one of my secret ambitions was to give them all a chance to play in the Royal Albert Hall, a place I have always loved to visit, having heard many fine concerts there. It seems to have a wonderful atmosphere and I also enjoy watching *The Last Night of the Proms* on television. I added that I knew it could only be a dream, as I could never

With Elizabeth Hunt and Philip Fowke — 1976
(Courtesy of Tiverton Gazette)

afford to hire it. As a small, unknown local youth orchestra, it was most unlikely we would ever be invited to take part in any kind of event there. Miss Graham seemed interested in what I was doing, but once the concert arrangements were finalised, I did not expect to hear from her again.

Elizabeth Hunt's appearance in 1976 was a tremendous success. The concert was held at the end of April at the Grammar School and once again we had a full house. As before, the Orchestra played for part of the programme and our guest for the second part of each half. She was accompanied by Philip Fowke who was, in fact, an accomplished soloist in his own right, having recently won the prestigious Leeds Piano Competition. I had left the booking to Miss Graham, who had not informed me of this, so he was rather piqued to find his name in much smaller letters on the posters than Miss Hunt's. Still, she was the star attraction as far as I was concerned!

The Royal Albert Hall

What activity can match conducting in fulfilment?
(Yehudi Menuhin)

Some time afterwards I was surprised to receive another call from Miss Graham, this time asking if I would be prepared to travel to London to meet a friend of hers, a Miss Herrod, who was in charge of bookings at the Royal Albert Hall. I had no real idea why they wanted to see me, but I went up to London and we met as arranged for a very enjoyable lunch at The Hilton.

A most exciting proposition was then put before me. There was a possibility of hiring the Hall for a very much smaller fee that normal, but there were of course several conditions attached to this. There are various levels of hire charges depending on a number of factors and it seemed there was a spare slot in April of the following year, when a huge Asian cultural festival was to be held. They required the Hall in the morning for a rehearsal and in the evening for their concert, but in the afternoon it would be free. It was not a space that would easily be filled, so if I agreed to call my concert a 'rehearsal' I could have it at the appropriate rate. However, the size of the audience would have to be limited, so they would not need to employ many staff to act as door stewards, etc.

Another condition was that as this was a very special concession I was not to tell anyone what the fee would be. I see, looking through old press cuttings of the event, that several of them mention a price, but they did not get this information from me and none of the sums were correct. I never told a soul. If you are hoping that I will at last reveal the secret, I am afraid you will be disappointed!

I returned to Tiverton in high spirits after this meeting and joyfully announced to my family that I had just hired the Royal Albert Hall for a concert to celebrate my 65th birthday in 1977, or as close as I could get to that date, which was actually May 29th. There was a stunned silence as they tried to absorb the news. After all, as Margaret later remarked, how many ordinary housewives are confronted with a husband who comes home with this sort of information? I told the orchestra what I was planning and sent them home with letters warning everyone to keep the date free at all costs. Then I told the local press – we had two newspapers, the Tiverton Gazette and the Devon and Somerset News – and it was promptly passed on to the Express and Echo in Exeter.

I didn't think that members' families alone would form a big enough audience to make it a special occasion, and wondered if the allocation of 200 seats would all be taken up. So I made the mistake of saying that anyone could come along. It did not occur to me that anyone outside Tiverton would be in the least interested in going all the way to London to hear us play.

It came as a real shock to find ourselves inundated with telephone calls from most of the national daily newspapers, TV stations and others – all demanding interviews and wanting further information about myself and the Orchestra. I gave them some details, but emphasised that this was a private event for our members, families and some of our regular supporters – adding, unwisely, that yes, there might after that be a few spare tickets.

The unlikely story of an amateur conductor of a Youth Orchestra, in a small town like Tiverton, daring to hire such a prestigious venue seemed to strike a note, if you will pardon the pun, and it was syndicated to newspapers all over the world. Soon I was receiving even more calls and letters, asking where they could obtain tickets, or telling me about their Devon connections. They came from America, Canada, New Zealand, Australia and other places. Some had relatives called Davey and wanted to know if we might be related. At the same time I began to hear from dozens of ex-members who wanted to be a part of this historic occasion. Soon I was sending packets of sheet music to them so they could start practising, because there would be no opportunity for a full rehearsal beforehand. After all, officially the concert *itself* was to be a rehearsal!

Meanwhile, I received a rather irate letter from a very worried Miss Herrod. She, also, was receiving a great deal of attention from the Press, and I think she was beginning to regret her generous gesture in allowing me to hire the Hall. She reminded me that I really could not have an unlimited number of people in the audience. I told her that I was well aware of that, but it seemed that the media, with their usual disregard for accuracy, had made reference to the normal seating capacity, which is about 10,000. Some articles implied that the event would be open to all, even though in any interviews I had given over the phone I had explained that it was not. I then told her that the orchestra itself was going to be bigger than originally planned, because of all the ex-members who wanted to come. I said it was going to be very difficult to keep to the original limit of 200 for our audience of family and supporters. Rather reluctantly, she agreed to increase this to 500, but made it clear that no more concessions would be made.

I arranged to have this number of special programmes printed, which would also serve as tickets. We allocated a certain number to each player and set aside some for special friends who I particularly wanted to be there. I still have a letter from Lord Amory, who was rather bewildered by the whole idea. He anxiously asked if I really wanted to do a concert in London, might I not have done better to hire a smaller hall, and in any case, how on earth was it to be paid for? I was able to assure him that the quite modest cost (considering it was the Royal Albert Hall) would be met entirely by myself and that I would not be seeking any financial help from him on this occasion! I tried to explain that it was not so much that I wanted a concert in London, but that I wanted one in this particular place, but he still sounded very dubious.

I then had to consider how we were all to get to London, and went down to see Mr S. Kingdom, of our local coach company, Kingdom's Tours. I arranged to hire virtually his entire fleet – eight coaches in all – with the remaining ticket holders making their own ways by car or train. Transport was very much cheaper in those days and I think we charged only £2 each for the coach fares. Our son John was by now at Bristol University, but naturally wanted to take part as a former member, and there were several others who needed to be picked up en route. Margaret devised a plan for this, which required careful timing and locations.

It is very hard to describe the tensions that were building up during this time. We were still having a great deal of media attention – and neither Margaret nor I had experienced anything like it, so we were finding it all rather overwhelming. We were still getting phone calls and letters from

PROGRAMME

TIVERTON YOUTH ORCHESTRA

PRESIDENT **VISCOUNT AMORY** CONDUCTOR **RONALD DAVEY**

JUBILEE CONCERT REHEARSAL

ROYAL ALBERT HALL, LONDON.

Friday 15th April 1977, at 2pm.

ANNOUNCERS

MR. R. LOCKYER MR. B. READE

THE QUEEN

Orchestra	The Radetsky March	*Strauss*
	Overture "Spring Tide"	*by Woodhouse*
Solo	Mr. S. Russell (Trumpet)	
Orchestra	Overture "The Diadem"	*Herman*
Solo	Mr. John Whitechurch (Tenor)	
Orchestra	The Entrance and March of the Peers	*Sullivan*
	The Strings of the Orchestra:–	
	Gavotte	*Bach*
	Intermezzo from Cavalleria Rusticana	*Mascanni*
Orchestra	Finlandia	*Sibelius*
Solo	Miss Heather Saunders (Piano)	
Orchestra	Farandole (from the L'Arlesienne suite)	*Bizet*

INTERVAL 20 minutes

Orchestra	Overture "The Caliph of Bagdad"	*Boiedieu*
Solo	Mr. D. Stone	
Duet	Mr. M. Hawkins and Mr. P. Waite, Solo Trumpets playing with orchestra Trumpet Tune & Air	*Purcell*
Duet	Miss B. Budge, (Piano) Miss T. Foster (Viola)	
Orchestra	The Finale from the 5th Symphony	*Beethoven*
Solo	Mr. G. Hills (Trombone)	
Orchestra	Suite No. 2. from the Water Music	*Handel*
Duet	Miss. Anne Rendell and Miss Clare Taylor Flute and Guitar	
Orchestra	Pictures at an Exhibition. Promenade , The Old Castle. Promenade, The Great Gate of Kiev.	*Moussorgsky*
Solo	Miss. Rosemary Davis	
Orchestra	The Pomp and Circumstance March Soloist: Mr. S. Mudge	*Elgar*

THE QUEEN

* *

This programme, PRICE £2.00 will include the coach to London and entrance to the Royal Albert Hall.

A Packed Lunch would be advisable.

Refreshments will be obtainable at the hall during the concert.

A collection will be made for the Musicians Benevolent Fund, and the Jacqueline Du Pré Appeal Fund for Research into Multiple Sclerosis.

people wanting tickets and we also had the transport and other details to arrange. I tried on my dress suit and discovered that the trousers did not fit properly, so I asked a family friend who was a retired tailor to alter them for me. All this time Margaret and I were still doing our job as Wardens, looking after 23 elderly tenants. I was busy holding extra rehearsals and making sure I had all the right music, while Margaret was still holding her weekly Brownie meetings – so it was a very hectic time for us.

Our daughter Jeanne was not an orchestra member at that time, but I needed someone to play tubular bells, which featured in one of our new pieces, Mussorgski's *The Great Gate of Kiev*. In fact, I did not even possess a set, as they are very expensive. Jeanne – never having even seen any, let alone knowing how they were played – should have known better than to say, "Well, Dad, if you can find a set, I'll play them for you."

I mentioned my need of this instrument at one of our rehearsals and one of the Town Band members, who also played with us, told me he knew of a set belonging to the Band. It was in very bad condition, languishing in the attic of the Town Hall, but never used. They willingly handed them over to me and so my startled daughter found me, one evening, on her doorstep with these filthy metal tubes, a very tatty broken wooden frame and damaged leather straps. Jeanne spent many hours patiently repairing and cleaning it all, until it looked like new. I also kept her to her promise about playing them. So now I had both my children involved, which made me very happy. After this, John gave her some lessons on the various instruments in the percussion section, passing on his own training, and Jeanne remained a regular member, also taking on much of the administration for a number of years. It was an enormous help to us all and we were very grateful. By this time Maureen Rendell found herself too busy to manage our accounts, so it all worked out very well.

April 15th, 1977! At last the great day dawned. I had a quick breakfast and packed up my dress suit trousers and a new, very smart beige lined jacket, a gift for the occasion from Mr John Soundy, whose son Michael was one of our percussionists. Margaret had bought me a carnation for my buttonhole, Malcolm Sargent-style. We set off for Fore Street, which was not yet pedestrianised, to find the fleet of coaches already there, waiting. Our larger instruments such as the tubular bells, double bass and drums had already been loaded onto one of them the evening before. Each coach was numbered, with one senior Orchestra member in charge and a list of those who were to be checked on and off at various stages of the journey. Margaret had undertaken to be on the bus designated to pick up various people en route and she prayed they would all be there on time. Fortunately this all went quite smoothly and there were no hitches.

Everyone was very excited when at last we arrived outside the Royal Albert Hall. Most of them had never seen it and were amazed by its size and style. We unloaded our instruments and were allowed to leave them inside. We had some free time before we would be able to go inside to prepare, so we all went off to find places to eat the picnic lunches we had brought. Some of us went and sat on the steps of the Albert Memorial, where some press photographers and a TV crew found us and took some pictures. Then it was back to the Hall and I began the mammoth task of setting out all the chairs and stands on the stage in the arrangement I wanted. I had plenty of offers of help, but the final responsibility was, as always, mine. I used to draw up a large plan before any big concert and I still have the one I made for this. There were 104 players in all, plus some soloists, so it was quite a task. Then all the music had to be put out on the right stands and I had a pile of spares in case I had miscounted.

By now our audience was beginning to filter in and Miss Herrod came in with the Hall's managing director, Mr Tony Charlton, to see that everything was all right. They were very nice to me, considering all the headaches I had caused them. They said they were still having trouble with the media and reminded me not to say a word about the fee, but I assured them I had told no one and never would. Lord Amory arrived and was settled into his front seat, still very bemused by the whole venture. The members had changed into their smart concert clothes and I must say they all looked quite splendid – I was really proud of them all. I then realised two things. One, I had left my carnation buttonhole at home, sitting in a vase in the kitchen, but, more disastrously, in my haste that morning I had packed the wrong pair of dress suit trousers and the ones I had brought were too long. Thus it was, that for the whole of the concert I was to be seen desperately hitching them up between items – something that seems to have been remembered by everyone who was there on that memorable day!

At the Royal Albert Hall — 15th April 1977

(Courtesy of The Guardian)

And so, the culmination of all my dreams! I stood on the conductor's rostrum, where so many famous figures had been before me, raised my baton, and everyone stood for the National Anthem. We had two announcers: my good friend of many years, Robert Lockyer, who had often compèred our concerts and Brian Reade, who had recently helped us so much with our French visit. Soon the hall was filled with the sound of our first piece, Strauss's rousing *Radetsky March*, and I knew that everything was going to be fine. In spite of the fact that some of the players had not rehearsed at all, they all blended in beautifully and although a few of the items were less than perfect, I think on the whole it sounded pretty good. The great thing was that everyone was obviously enjoying every moment. A full list of all those who took part can be found at the end of this book.

Not very long before the concert, I was asked by Jon Sowden, an old school friend of my daughter, if I would like a recording of the whole thing, because he had a friend who was willing to help to do this and, naturally, I agreed. Recording equipment was not as common or as sophisticated as it is now, but he and his friend Mr Alvin Ellacott did a very good job and this was eventually to provide us with a lasting souvenir of the day.

Just before the last item Lord Amory came forward to say a few words and to present me with two gifts on behalf of the orchestra. One was a collection of records by Yehudi Menuhin, in two boxes, the inner sleeves of which, I later discovered, had been actually signed by him. One of the members had written, unknown to me, to invite him to attend. This he was unable to do, but he had readily agreed to sign the covers. The other gift was in a smaller package and Lord Amory humorously expressed the hope that it might contain a pair of braces, which I was obviously in need of! In fact, it was a silver cup, engraved with the date and the occasion and as it was the year of the Queen's Silver Jubilee, this was commemorated on the other side.

I said a few words of thanks to everyone, including the long-suffering Hall management and called Margaret onto the stage to be thanked for all the work she had done for me. At that point I was astonished to see an entire TV film crew appear, headed by a well-known top reporter of the time, Keith Hatfield, who proceeded to interview me there and then. Rather than feeling flattered, I must admit that my first reaction was to be rather irritated by the interruption to what had been, until then, a very smooth programme. I remember answering a few of his questions, but when he asked how much I had paid for the Hall, I politely declined to say. He persisted, quite forcibly until I replied, "It's none of your damned business and I'm not going to tell you!" I then told him that we had only a short time left in which to finish our final item, as we had to be out of the Hall by five o'clock and they would have to go. He and the crew meekly left the stage, although they did remain in the Hall to shoot some more film.

My final announcement to the audience was to tell them that our next concert would be in Cadeleigh Village Hall – it was not actually true, but most of the audience were from Tiverton and appreciated the contrast, so it made everyone laugh!

In true *Last Night of the Proms* fashion, we closed with Elgar's *Pomp and Circumstance March*, with the vocal part being taken by Stephen Mudge from Blundell's School. One more rendering of the National Anthem and it was all over.

All that remained was the usual clearing up of music and instruments and time – just – to have a few words with some of our past members who had travelled to London from all over the country especially for the occasion and whom I had not seen for a long time.

We piled back into our coaches for the return journey, stopping on the way for some much-needed refreshments. Later, unfortunately, three of the coaches broke down. I rather suspect that some older ones had been pressed into service in somewhat less than perfect condition, and mine was among them. As we stopped on the hard shoulder of the motorway, a police patrol officer came to tell us to stay on the coach until a replacement arrived, although it was to be quite a long wait.

On seeing me, the policeman exclaimed, "I know you! I've just seen you on the TV! You're Ron Davey and the Tiverton Youth Orchestra!" It seemed that we had featured quite prominently on the evening news, but as I was stuck on the motorway, I never did see it, although I was sent a copy of part of the programme. For some time afterwards I received letters from friends who had seen it and were highly amused at the way I told Keith Hatfield to mind his own business!

Much more recently the same film clips were twice included in a TV programme called *Today's the Day* in which contestants were asked to identify news items from previous years – so they are evidently still in the archives.

The 'Royal Albert Hall' cake with Trevor Chilcott (longest serving TYO member)

Soon after our return, Jon Sowden telephoned me to say that the recording sounded quite good, in spite of a few technical difficulties. I had commissioned a local bakery, owned by Mr John Rendell, to make me a cake in the shape of the Royal Albert Hall and our original intention was to cut this after the performance. For several reasons, this was not possible, so I hired the Heathcoat Hall a week later for a party to celebrate our achievement, which was a wonderful way to round everything off. Jon and Mr Ellacott agreed to play the recording for us all to hear and everyone contributed a plate or two of food towards the refreshments. The wonderful cake was inevitably cut, though I still have the piece of icing which represented the Hall foyer! I should say that although I ordered the cake with the intention of paying for it, Mr Rendell very kindly gave it as a donation.

Even now, years later, former members and those who were in the audience tell me how thrilled they were to have had the chance to be a part of it all and I rather doubt if many of our soloists, good as they were, would ever have performed there otherwise.

During the party, someone suggested that we had a proper record made of the concert, using the tape recording, so I began to make enquiries and found a firm in London who thought that they could help. I sent the tape to them and though at first they said it was not quite up to the sound quality they normally needed, they finally agreed to produce a record for us. Margaret and I went to their London studios and we had a good discussion and agreed a price. For the sleeve, we chose a group photograph of the whole orchestra, taken at the concert. In due course a large parcel of records arrived which were soon selling well.

Many years later, while browsing in a local jumble sale, I found one on the white elephant stall. I was so sad to see it there that I bought it for 10p and later you will find out what I did with it!

The Hofheim Akkordeon Orchester (1950)

The music in my heart I bore
Long after it was heard no more

(From *The Reaper*, by Wordsworth)

Well! How to follow that? Never one to rest on my laurels, I decided to seriously consider the invitation I had been given to take the Orchestra to Hofheim. I wrote to Herr Günter Powils and there followed a series of letters. Mine were in English and his in German, for neither of us could speak a word of each other's language. Mr Brian Richards, the language teacher at Blundell's School, was very kind in translating this early correspondence and there was help available at the other end. Even so, there were a number of minor misunderstandings, but in due course a date was set and I began to make arrangements, assisted by Margaret and Jeanne. I told the orchestra members what was being planned and we began another series of fund-raising events. Fortunately, at that time we had an excellent group of supportive parents. Many of them organised various enterprises quite independently of myself, so we had jumble sales, a meat bingo, street busking – all kinds of things going on, which helped enormously. I arranged another sponsored play-in, this time in an empty shop in Fore Street, now part of the NatWest Bank. I hoped to be able to subsidise the cost for our members as much as possible, as I knew from my own family how hard it can be for parents to afford these trips, especially where there is more than one child wanting to go.

At this time, Tiverton was not yet twinned with Hofheim, although officials of both towns had met through our common link with Chinon. I know that the German government was then very keen to promote such ventures, in an effort, I am sure, to try to overcome the bad feelings that rather understandably still existed in some quarters following the Second World War. Even after nearly thirty years, people had long memories. Perhaps family members had died in battle or suffered from air raids – and the dreadful revelations that came to light afterwards regarding the concentration camps were not forgotten. Of course, I too hated the Nazi regime and all it stood for and would have died for my country during the war or, indeed, at any time. But I felt now that the only way forward was to get the young people of all nations to know each other as fellow human beings. If they could visit each other in their homes and get to know something of their cultures it might be a step towards international understanding – it could even, in time, lead to a more peaceful and tolerant world. This generation had not even been born when the war began.

I knew that even as I planned this visit there were Tiverton people who strongly disapproved of the idea, and I could only hope they would come to understand why I was doing it.

A number of parents enquired if perhaps they could come too, so I wrote to Hofheim and asked if accommodation could be found for them in local guesthouses or small hotels, for which, of course, each extra visitor would pay on arrival. Everyone else would stay in the homes of their members or other local families.

The number of those wanting to go with us kept growing until we realised that we would need two coaches, with a total of almost 100 people. I never seem to do things by halves!

By this time poor Herr Powils, his wife Ingrid and the other senior members of the Hofheim Akkordeon Orchester (1950) – to give them their full title – were beginning to feel overwhelmed by the whole project. I expect, like myself, they were wondering just how we had managed to start this, back in the caves of Chinon, where the wine had flowed so freely…..!

At that point they appealed to their local council for assistance, which was readily forthcoming. They were most anxious that we should receive a warm welcome and perhaps pave the way for a three-way twinning, which was evidently their hope. Tiverton's Mayor and Mayoress at the time were Cllr and Mrs Derek Coulthard who were to be among the party, but as yet had no brief from the people of Tiverton to agree to any kind of alliance with Hofheim.

We sent a list of all our members and supporters together with the programmes of music we intended to play for a major concert in their Town Hall and some smaller ones, including two at local retirement homes.

So, once again we faced a long journey to our destination, this one even longer than to Chinon. It was late afternoon and everyone was very

TYO members first visit to Hofheim — 1977

tired by the time we reached the magnificent Town Hall in Hofheim, where a smiling group, led by Günter and Ingrid Powils, greeted us.

We all scrambled off the coaches and into the foyer. Our hosts were holding some papers with the lists of host families and after a few formal words of welcome they proceeded to call out names, and people came forward to claim their guests, some of whom looked a bit apprehensive as they were whisked away, each clutching a small packet containing a very precise programme for our visit and other useful information. We watched as our daughter Jeanne and her husband Mike went off with a smiling gentleman and his two teenage daughters. I was later told that this family had thought they were getting two brothers, not a husband and wife, and perhaps the girls had hoped to meet up with a pair of nice eligible young English boys! It was after this that my daughter decided to change the spelling of her name from Jean to Jeanne, to avoid future confusion! However, the Weck family was very kind and Jeanne stayed with them again on a later visit.

Those staying in guesthouses and hotels went next, taken by one of our own coaches and then there only remained a small number including Margaret and myself. We were told that, as there were not enough places with local families for us all, we were to stay in the Landsberg Hotel. This was a famous historical site, having been the place where a treaty was negotiated to end the Thirty Years War. The language barrier began to cause problems at once, because at this point we were uncertain if we would be expected to pay for the hotel ourselves. Some of our group were very worried because they had not brought enough money for such expenses, but I promised that I would sort everything out and they seemed happier. We were to be taken to local families for our evening meal, but would return to the hotel to sleep. Hans-Jürgen Mock, the young man I had met in Chinon, collected Margaret and I and took us to his home. Marianne, his mother, greeted us, but his father, Karl-Heinz, was away from home in a sanatorium with a chest problem. We were given a warm welcome and an excellent meal, for which we had a very good appetite. Hans-Jürgen had to work very hard for us that evening as our interpreter; his mother spoke no English and we had many questions to ask and be asked in return. Finally, tired but well fed, we returned to the hotel. This time we walked the short distance with Hans-Jürgen as our guide. He explained that the next evening we would have to find our own way to his home for our meal.

We fell into bed, exhausted, but neither of us could sleep much. I hoped we did not have too many problems ahead and wished very much that I could speak German! Next day, somewhat to my relief I was introduced to a gentleman who was to act as interpreter for our visit – his name was Klaus Giesen and he was to become a very good friend for many years. He was able to reassure us that our hotel was being paid for by their Town Council, so we had no need to worry on that score.

Our first morning was free, so Margaret decided she would like to do a trial run at finding the Mock family's house in daylight, rather than wait until evening. We carefully retraced our given route from the hotel and Margaret jotted down the names of the streets as we went. She noted one curious thing – there seemed to be two streets with the same name, though not connected, as there was a different one in between. Later that evening, at dinner, she asked Hans-Jürgen about it. He was puzzled at first, until she showed him her notebook where she had copied down what she had read. Then he laughed. She had written 'Einbahnstrasse' – which is German for 'one-way street'!

Our first concert was in the convalescent home – Kurhaus – of a small spa town, of which there are many in that part of Germany. It was a bit of a disappointment because, apart from our own non-playing friends from England and a few of the Hofheim organisers, hardly anyone was there. At the end, the manager presented me with a huge bouquet, and we consoled ourselves that at least it was a sort of extra rehearsal for us all! We next played in two retirement homes, the Martha Elsa Haus and the Marie Elisabeth Haus, where the elderly residents clearly enjoyed our visit. At the second a very old gentleman was given the task of welcoming us in English, the only person in the place able to do so and he was very proud of his ability. After each of these concerts we sent round some of our youngest members with tins of Roses chocolates, as we had done in Chinon, and were, in turn, given some light refreshments.

In addition to the concerts, a very full programme had been planned for us, including visits to various local places of interest, taking in, of course, a tour of the historical parts of Hofheim itself. Many old houses were being restored very tastefully, showing many exposed beams – typical of the area – and much like our old English Tudor buildings. Since this first visit we have seen many more restorations and improvements to the town as part of their ongoing programme of works.

After the tour of the town, the mayor, Herr Flaccus, gave us an official reception in the Town Hall. One day the older members of the party were taken to an apfelwein (cider) factory, where we had generous free samples to wash down some delicious wurst (sausages) with chunks of crusty bread. The younger ones had been taken to a Coca Cola plant and were equally well treated – but they greatly resented not being allowed to come with the rest of us and have cider! One evening, however, there was a big party for all of us plus the host families and there was plenty of apfelwein served there, but mostly of the non-alcoholic kind! During the week we came to know several more of the orchestra's officials, including Herr Kurt Erdniss, who helped with the administration, and Frau Diethild Kyritz, who trained the junior section. There were also, as with our own Orchestra, a number of parents who took an interest and came with us on our various outings and generally gave assistance where required.

We had sent programmes for our concerts in advance and I had given, as asked, approximate timings, which were approved by our hosts. I was therefore rather taken aback when Frau Kyritz informed me, quite brusquely, that the programme for the final, main concert was too long and she then proceeded to tell me which items were to be cut!

Now, anyone who has not planned a programme for a Youth Orchestra may not understand that there is far more to this than one might think. These are not professionals, nor in many cases, very skilled players and it is not just a question of picking a selection of suitable music. Some of our pieces had short solo passages for a particular instrument, ideal for young players to show off their skills, although they were perhaps not yet quite ready to tackle a whole solo spot. It is an encouragement and those chosen for these little cameos would take them very seriously and practice hard at this small chance to shine – and to leave out their moment of glory would have been a great disappointment to them. Some of our pieces were better rehearsed and we would not have wanted to omit our best ones. Then, if an item has a great deal of work for the wind and brass sections, they would need a respite afterwards, so a piece that is mainly strings will be put in next, to give them a breather – children have a more limited lung capacity than adults. Finally, we had lugged our enormous set of tubular bells along specially for our 'pièce de resistance' – *The Great Gate of Kiev* as played in the Royal Albert Hall – and were certainly not about to leave that one out!

Obviously, I did not want to fall out with our hosts, who had gone to so much trouble to entertain us and whom we had pressed to the limit with our very large numbers – and I am sure I could have explained but for the language problem. Frau Kyritz could speak English, but not as well as Herr Giesen. I very firmly pointed out that they had had plenty of time to tell me the programme was too long, but now we were here, we intended to play all of it.

Frau Kyritz seemed rather startled by my stance and went into a huddle with the others, while I went and found Herr Giesen and tried to explain why I was not prepared to alter our programme. He went over to join the discussion and nothing further was said on the matter. I am happy to say we have all remained the best of friends.

Our main concert was held on the eve of our departure in their large and very grand Stadthalle (Town Hall). To our surprise, it was not laid out with the audience in rows, but with long tables, set at right angles to the stage, at which the audience sat. Waitresses went around serving refreshments and drinks throughout the evening. I have to say, I found this rather distracting at first, but it was less of a problem than I feared and I soon became used to it.

Since meeting the Akkordeon Orchester in France, they had acquired a new conductor and we were introduced just before we began; his name was Herr Josef Dieser. With him was his wife, Karin, who was one of the players. They played for the first part of the programme, there were various speeches during the interval with an official exchange of suitable gifts, and we played for the second half.

The concert went well. We had some solos by Chris Martin accompanied by Paul Matthews of Blundell's School, who was there with his wife, Pam. Chris and his family happened to be in Europe at the time and he had brought his older son, Simon, with him to join us for a few days. We also had a couple of duets from Claire Taylor and her friend Anne Rendell, daughter of Roy and Maureen.

Our finale was a rendering of *Land of Hope and Glory*, and our English supporters in the audience were so overcome by the reception we had received and the whole atmosphere (and perhaps also by the local beer and wine?) that they rose as one to sing along with us. The bewildered German audience followed suit, assuming it was some sort of English tradition. It was rather odd to see them all standing to our very patriotic song!

We sold quite a few of our Royal Albert Hall records afterwards and then, tired as we were, began to pack everything up ready for a very early departure next morning.

The concert had been quite long and it was late. Getting back to the hotel and our comfortable beds was really the only thought in our minds! But it was not to be. An official invitation had been issued by the Mayor to our own Mayor and Mayoress, Cllr and Mrs Coulthard, and we were also included, together with a few of our committee. Naturally, an invitation of that sort cannot be refused, so we all trooped down to the restaurant underneath the Stadthalle. We ate very little, being too tired to feel hungry, but the reason for the meeting soon became clear. One of the officials at that time was a Dr Bussman, who had a charming, but very forceful personality. He began enthusiastically demanding that an agreement to form an official twinning between our towns be made there and then. Derek Coulthard tried in vain to explain that however keen we all might be, he had no authority from Tiverton to agree to this, although he promised to put the idea forward on his return. Dr Bussman became even more pressing and I rather think it was a very important political issue at that time for their town. Eventually Margaret came to Derek's rescue with an inspired analogy.

"Imagine," she explained, "a shy young girl, being courted by a handsome young man. She certainly likes him, but they have only just met. So, when the young man proposes marriage, she hesitates and replies, 'Perhaps – but not just yet. You must give me a little time to get to know you.'" Everyone laughed, the tension was broken and soon afterwards we made our way back to the hotel and, thankfully, our beds.

The desired twinning did not take place for some time, however. When Cllr Mrs Eileen Trickey became Mayor she called a public meeting to ascertain the town's wishes and eventually, in 1980, it became official, with the signing of formal charters. There began many exchange visits by different organisations in both directions and, of course, by our own Twinning Committee which still works very hard to maintain links with both Hofheim and Chinon.

Next morning at a horribly early hour we assembled outside the Stadthalle and loaded everything onto the coaches before saying our farewells to the Akkordeon Orchester officials and the families who had come to see us off. By the time we had all walked the long line of our new friends, exchanging last-minute presents and goodbye hugs, there were few dry eyes.

We extended a return invitation for the following year and in fact over the years, returned four more times with the Youth Orchestra, the last one in 1996 arranged not by myself but my successor, Wilf Saunders. Margaret and I were also fortunate enough to visit Hofheim with the Twinning Committee several times and once on a private visit. Each time we were guests of our very good friends, the Mock family.

In return we hosted four visits by the Hofheim Akkordeon Orchester, with a private visit from Herr and Frau Mock and Kurt Erdniss. We also entertained several other people during visits arranged by the Twinning Committee and also the Town Band.

Hofheim Akkordeon Orchester's first visit to England — May 1978

(Courtesy of Tiverton Gazette)

The first time the Hofheim Orchester came to Tiverton was in May 1978 and we had plenty of support from all kinds of sources. Paul Matthews of Blundell's School managed to get us the free use of their big concert hall, so we did not need not make a charge for admission and thus ensured a nice big audience for their first visit. He also arranged an afternoon's entertainment for them before the concert, which everyone enjoyed very much, and which left me free for other things.

Two other teachers from the school helped with a guided walk around the town, which happily coincided with Mayor's Sunday. Mr Brian Jenkins gave one of his fascinating historical talks, while Mr Brian Richards translated. Lady Amory, in person, very kindly took them around the gardens at Knightshayes. Apparently some of the German youngsters had expected her to be wearing a coronet as she escorted them round, instead of a headscarf! Afterwards, Lord Amory kindly treated everyone to a cream tea in the restaurant.

Soon after our first visit to Germany, Margaret resolved to try to learn some of the language, as she felt at such a disadvantage, being unable to communicate. She attended evening classes at East Devon College and though she says she can't manage anything too complicated, she now copes quite well with basic conversation and enjoyed the challenge. It certainly came in very handy on later visits when a couple of members had to be taken to the local hospital and also when dealing with some of the correspondence.

Once, we made all the arrangements for a party of teenage musicians from the Hofheim School of Music, which involved finding them accommodation, places to play and outings. This was a bit fraught, as we did not get on well with their teacher who was very demanding and not very appreciative of our efforts. They had asked to visit for a week, but this somehow stretched into ten days and many of our friends who were kindly acting as hosts were understandably feeling a little put upon. The young players themselves were quite gifted, playing classical guitars, flutes and recorders, but as we were already quite busy enough arranging exchanges with the Akkordeon Orchester, I asked Herr Giesen not to involve us again with this group.

I will not go into too much detail about all our exchange visits; after a time they developed a similar form each time, with minor variations. The host orchestra would arrange accommodation with families for the visitors, and a full programme of concerts and outings. Usually there would be an official reception in our respective Town Halls and always a good party for everyone – guests, hosts and orchestra members who had been unable to have a guest. One year we had a disco at the Tiverton Hotel, but mostly we had an old-fashioned evening with games and a spot of country dancing, devised by Wilf and his son David, who were excellent at this. One year, the Hofheim people gave us a concert of their latest Carnival Club's production – a hilarious take-off of various British traditions. I particularly remember our friend Karl-Heinz Mock dancing around in a kilt, which kept falling down!

A popular feature of their later parties was a contraption that fired chocolate marshmallows into the air, which you had to try to catch. It was great fun, if rather messy at times!

There was a lot of administration work to be done, whether we were visiting or hosting. Jeanne and Margaret, together with several of the adult members, coped with all this and left me free to sort out the concerts.

We always tried to arrange for both orchestras to play at least one piece all together and it was sometimes quite hard to find something suitable.

With Josef Dieser, conductor of the Hofheim Akkordeon Orchester, at a private party in his home

One year it was Beethoven's *Hymn of Joy*. More than once it was a composition by Josef Dieser, which he had kindly dedicated to us, called *Hello Friends* – a lively piece which became one of our favourites.

We had a few glitches from time to time, of course, but generally things went quite well, especially as we all became more experienced. One mishap occurred when we were returning across Dartmoor from a visit to Plymouth. Their driver misunderstood our directions, took the wrong turning, and a narrow bridge made it impossible for the large German coach to continue. There was nothing else to do but turn around and go back to the crossroads to pick up the correct route. This made us very late indeed getting back, so we had to phone Tiverton with a message for waiting families. Meanwhile, I decided to entertain them with a few of our old local folk legends, including *The Hairy Hand*, which is supposed to steer unwary travellers off the road. Herr Giesen translated this with great dramatic effect and everyone was very amused. Later they made a video of their visit and included a realistic model of a large, green hairy hand manhandling a bus!

More trouble with Ron's braces!
At a social evening with Hofheim friends
Klaus Giesen and Günter Powils — England 1980
(Courtesy of Castle Photographers)

1980 was a special year for them, being their 30th anniversary, and they asked if we could arrange a really special concert. Because they had heard all about our Royal Albert Hall concert, they asked if that would be possible, but it would have been far too great an undertaking and there would have been no price concession this time!

Eventually we thought about the University Great Hall in Exeter and found that it would be possible. It turned out to be a huge success, as it was well publicised and we had a very good audience. Among them were members of the Sidmouth Accordion Orchestra, who made a large block booking. On a later visit by the Hofheim orchestra they helped us by putting on a venue in Sidmouth for a concert and also gave them a meal beforehand.

The University Hall was quite expensive to hire and we were told that if we remained on the premises at all after 11 pm there would be a hefty additional charge.

Knowing our Hofheim friends' fondness for long speeches, Margaret told them that the deadline was 10.30 pm. By the time we had cleared the hall it was 10.45 pm – so we were all right! As we drove home, Karl-Heinz Mock, who was, as always, our guest with his wife Marianne, asked anxiously how much extra the hall would cost and offered, as their Treasurer to make a contribution. Margaret laughed and explained what she had done and he was most amused at our subterfuge. In fact we made a modest profit, so all was well.

Margaret and I [centre] with Karl-Heinz Mock and Marianne, our host family — Hofheim 1981

Our choice of sightseeing trips included a guided tour of Wells, by courtesy of David Chivers, who had initially become involved as a parent, but later acted as one of our regular compères. We went to Cheddar Caves, The Valley of Rocks, Lyme Regis (where we started off in gorgeous sunshine and ended in a massive thunderstorm). We had a lovely day at Cricket St Thomas Wildlife Park and another time we took them to the Elizabethan Fair at Totnes, where some of them dressed up in medieval German costumes and played their accordions in the square. This was arranged for us by the Totnes Elizabethan Society, who also gave us a guided tour and plenty of free cups of tea.

In return, we had visits to several splendid theme parks in Germany, Phantasialand being the last and far the biggest, a cross between Disneyland and Alton Towers. I must mention our visits to Rüdesheim, on the Rhine, a rather touristy little place, but very pretty for all that. There we were taken, on two occasions, to a fascinating museum of mechanical musical machines and shown around by the owner, a wonderfully eccentric character called Siegfried, who wore a huge black hat, enormous baggy trousers and a string vest.

One year, Günter Powils and I decided to add a bit of humour into the main concert by having a few of us dress up as gypsies and come into the hall as a band of strolling players. Marianne had great fun kitting me out in a frilly blouse from the Carnival Club store and a kerchief on my head, but my large false moustache came adrift during my solo rendering of *Czardas* – a lively gypsy piece – which caused even more laughter.

Dressed up as gypsies

One year, our Chairman, Mr Reg Tayler composed a piece of music called *Ceremonial March,* and this was presented to their orchestra and played at a concert.

We have had some very loyal supporters on both sides; Cllr Mrs Eunice Hann and her husband, Eddie accommodated a whole group of young boys several times, while her own sons were involved as members and went with us to Hofheim more than once. Mr Peter Hambleton, for many years Chairman of Tiverton Twinning Association was also a great help. He and his wife, Barbara, also hosted extra guests for us and became good friends of ours. Sadly, Peter died in 1994 after a short illness and we still miss him very much. David and Sheila Chivers were another couple who came to our rescue with spare beds when needed and helped in many other ways.

Over in Hofheim, Herr and Frau Füller could usually be relied upon to take a group of our members, in spite of having a severely handicapped daughter. A 'larger than life' character, he quickly made friends with his first host family, the Stains, whose daughter Melanie was a regular member and they, like several others, did some private exchange visits in addition to the official ones. Kurt Erdniss became a good friend of ours and still sends us gifts of wine and other German specialities from time to time. He always took us out for a meal whenever we were over there, and still remembers our birthdays. He is a great philosopher and his letters are full of profound observations on life in general as well as all the news from Hofheim.

Of course, what with having other Hofheim guests from time to time, we came to know quite a lot of people and it was always difficult, if not impossible, to fit in all the invitations we received whenever we visited the town. We always stayed with the Mock family, who acted as our 'social secretaries' on these occasions, sorting out which friends we could manage to fit in and making tactful excuses to the others. There were invitations for 'kaffee und kuchen' in the mornings and afternoons, lunch and evening parties – all most enjoyable, though the generous slices of rich cream cakes did not do a lot for our figures!

Herr Flaccus and his successor Herr Felix, as Burgermeisters, were always most kind and we were once included in a group invited to a very smart restaurant for a superb lunch.

During all these exchanges Klaus Giesen coined a motto for us all, which we regularly used in our publicity. It was, 'Music knows no boundaries'. I think this is an excellent sentiment.

It was during the 1980s that the Post Office began to replace their familiar red telephone boxes with modern new booths, and many people were asking to buy the old ones as they were removed. We had a letter from Herr Powils saying that they had had a brilliant idea! They wanted one of these old phone boxes to be a gift from our two organisations to the Hofheim Twinning Association. It was agreed that they would pay for the box itself and that we would get it and ship it to Hofheim, where it would be erected in the town to mark the official Twinning.

I made enquiries and found there was a long waiting list, so it was some time later (after several reminders to make sure we had not been forgotten) that we finally received a letter saying there was a box we could have. Then came a flurry of activity as we had to arrange some rather complicated official export paperwork, transportation and payment. Mr Mike Fitzpatrick (the father of one of our members, Heidi) worked at that time at Whitbread's in Tiverton and he was able to arrange a lorry and pallet to collect it from the Exeter Post Office depot and also take it to London. Someone from our Twinning Committee arranged a place there for it to be stored briefly while awaiting collection. Ingrid Powils, who worked for Polar Mohr, a large firm near Hofheim, persuaded them to collect it from London and transport it to Hofheim. Eventually it all fell into place and there were no hitches.

This old phone box now has pride of place and a plaque near the old Rathaus, right in the centre of Hofheim. Both our orchestras are very proud of the part we played in this venture. It is, in fact, a working telephone connected to the German network, but a few of the older residents thought you could only use it to speak to someone in England!

An English souvenir for Hofheim Günter and Ingrid Powils and their son, Jens — 1984

Alright on the Night!

At Last – Fortissimo!

(Mahler, on first seeing Niagara Falls)

I had long wanted to have a go at Tchaikovski's *1812 Overture*, but although I tried several times, it was not until 1978 that I believed it might be possible. We rehearsed for some time until I decided that we were almost ready for a really big performance, involving as many local musical groups as possible.

Once again I enlisted the co-operation of Paul Matthews of Blundell's School. He agreed to allow some of their school orchestra and military band, both of a very high standard, to join us – and the Headmaster, Mr Clive Gimpson, readily agreed to lend us their hall. I approached the Tiverton Town Band, several of whom played with us anyway, and they were very keen to take part. Then I wrote to all the local junior schools, inviting their recorder groups to come along as well. Each group rehearsed separately for most of the time, but at last we came together for a joint run-through. It was quite a headache making sure everyone had the right music and knew where to sit or stand.

I wanted some special effects to represent the cannon fire, which is, of course, an important feature of the piece. One of Blundell's School's science teachers, Mr Alan Furse, often came along to play the cello with us, so I asked him if he would arrange this. He purchased some special detonators and stage explosives and devised a system of setting them off at the right times, but of course it was not going to be possible to rehearse this part. We would have to trust that it would be 'alright on the night'!

The concert finally took place in February 1979, with a full audience and an equally full complement of players, which looked most impressive. The concert also featured items from the Heathcoat Junior School Choir; the Blundell's School Choir; some piano solos by one of our own members, Russell Ayre; and other orchestral pieces. The *1812 Overture* itself, as the highlight of the evening, was every bit as successful as I had dreamed. Even though we had had few chances to rehearse as one, everything blended in well and the sheer volume of sound was, to me, quite wonderful.

The part that didn't quite go as planned, but caused great hilarity, was the 'special effects'. The first three explosions for the 'cannon fire' went off perfectly, but there must have been a fault with one of the remaining detonators, because the next one somehow set off the remaining ones as well. The resulting series of explosions were so incredibly loud that everyone, including myself, thought for a moment that we had blown up the school!

Apparently, one elderly lady near the front fell off her chair in surprise and several small children, terrified, burst into tears. An ominous cloud of smoke began to emerge from the small ante-room just off-stage where the detonators had been placed and Margaret, who was sitting next to Mr Gimpson, whispered to him that she hoped nothing had been damaged. He smiled reassuringly, but looked a bit anxious. The thick smoke billowed across the back of the stage. The percussion section, which included our daughter, lost sight of me and their music completely for a while and had to play entirely by ear, hoping that they were keeping in time with the rest of the orchestra. However, they valiantly played on, coughing only slightly, to the end of the piece.

The small children from the junior schools were highly entertained and thought the whole thing very exciting! When the concert was over, I went to find out what had happened and found several ceiling tiles in the ante-room blackened and broken and a strong smell like spent fireworks. I must say that Mr Gimpson took it very well and refused my offer to pay for the damage.

Later in 1979, at one of our concerts, I was presented with a gold watch from the Viscount Amory Trust, in recognition of my work with the orchestra. Our president, Lord Amory, was ill, so Mr Leslie Duffield, one of the Trustees, made the presentation in his place.

In 1981 we were deeply saddened to learn of the death of Lord Amory. His encouragement had always been highly valued by the orchestra and of course myself. He would be greatly missed by us all. Some time later I approached his nephew, Sir Ian Amory, and he kindly agreed to take on the role of President. He and Lady Amory have continued to provide the same support and interest and, in spite of their very busy lives, often attended our concerts.

During the 1980s we were invited to join in several Youth Concerts at the Barnfield Theatre in Exeter. These were arranged by the East Devon and Community Youth Service and would involve a number of local youth groups who would perform instrumental items, singing, dancing, sketches and so on. It was so crowded backstage that once we had done our part we would have to leave, so we were never able to stay and see the rest of the show, but I understand they were always very good. As a special treat for our members, Jeanne used to order a fish and chip supper from Capel's in Heavitree Road, Exeter, which we would collect on our way home. Everyone enjoyed this!

With granddaughter Emma, aged 3
TYO Christmas concert — 1986

Another regular event at this time would be a joint Christmas concert with the Heathcoat Junior School choir who were trained by their headteacher, Miss Edna Rodgers.

My granddaughter Emma eventually became a keen member of this choir and found her love of music and singing.

Sometimes these concerts were held in St Paul's Church, but once or twice they took place in St Peter's Church and occasionally in the William Shapland School (once the Tiverton Grammar School, now The Castle School). It was always rather more convenient to have one there, where we rehearsed, and all our instruments and stands were readily to hand and did not need transporting.

It used to take me hours to get everything in place, even shifting heavy pews in the churches, to make room for the choir to stand at the front – and I rarely had much help. We would give any money we raised to the church where we played or to a charity.

One year we did the same sort of thing, but with a choir from the Caroline Brewin School instead. It was always a pleasure to hear their young voices, and they were so obviously enjoying their singing. I think they liked hearing the orchestra, too. Some of them would never otherwise have attended any of our concerts, nor probably would their parents, so we reached another part of the community in this way.

We played for two or three National Children's Homes Festivals, a Civic Service at St Peter's Church with the then newly formed Middle Schools' Choir and the Tiverton Singers, both under their trainer and conductor, Mrs Marilyn Felix. Later, she went on to form the Tiverton Songsters (a junior choir) and then Tiverton Cantabile, a youth choir which reached a very high standard. We also held a joint concert with the Vibette dancers and Tiverton Majorettes, then under the guidance of Mrs Vera Gooding, who taught dancing to several generations of Tiverton children. I remember the girls in their red and white costumes marching around the New Hall to our theme tune, *Hello Friends*.

In between all this we did countless smaller concerts for various churches and charities – too many to list – and still found time to have the occasional social event for our members, usually a disco or party.

In 1982, to celebrate my 70th birthday, I invited Christopher Martin to give a Celebrity Concert at Blundell's School. This event proved to be a great success. He always manages to include a few interesting anecdotes and amusing stories, explaining the items he plays to the audience in a most engaging way. A concert with Christopher as soloist is always a pleasurable and relaxed occasion.

In 1985 his own students' orchestra, The Chamber Strings of Melbourne, were planning a tour of Europe and it was agreed that we would arrange a concert for them here in Tiverton, with hospitality overnight. We had no problem in finding families from among our members willing to take one or two of the young players, while the adults made their own arrangements to stay at the Tiverton Hotel. It was a most enjoyable evening and all the visitors were very pleasant and friendly.

They have since done several further European tours and won a prestigious trophy in Vienna.

We also hosted a Youth Band from Swindon. One of their organisers came from Tiverton and asked if we would provide a concert venue and a tea, but they did not need accommodation as they were staying in Exeter. Once again, members and parents rose to the occasion and a generous supply of refreshments appeared as if by magic.

Christopher Martin — 1980s

A Great Honour

And the rightful owner of the music,
tiny and no longer timid,
sang for the rightful owners of the song

(Brian Patten)

Early in 1982 I received a letter from the Prime Minister's office in Downing Street. I could not imagine what it might be. On opening it I found I had been nominated to receive an MBE for my services to the Youth Orchestra. I was warned that nothing should be said to anyone at all until it was announced officially with the Queen's Birthday Honours List.

The previous summer, Margaret and I had been invited to attend a Royal Garden Party and I thought that a great enough honour in itself, but this was something I had never imagined. Margaret and I kept the secret for quite a long time. We did not even confide in our children, for fear that they might let something slip; we had heard rumours that if it did get out, the honour would be cancelled! It was not until a couple of days before the announcement, when our son, daughter and son-in-law happened to be with us for the day, that we finally broke our silence.

Soon afterwards, of course, it was in all the papers and my orchestra members were full of congratulations. I told them I was accepting it on their behalf, because of all the hard work they put into their music. One wag suggested that it was, presumably, my 'Good *Conduct* Medal'!

Margaret made me a large 'temporary medal' out of a cheese box covered in foil as a joke, but it was to be October before I finally went up to London to receive the real one from Her Majesty the Queen.

We travelled to London by first-class coach, for which tickets had been sent. Our son, John, arrived separately from Bristol and we all stayed overnight at the Scout headquarters, Baden Powell House, through Margaret's Guiding connections. Next morning, dressed to kill in a morning dress suit, complete with top hat, courtesy of Moss Bros. and accompanied by my equally smart family, we drove by taxi to the gates of

Buckingham Palace. We arrived well before the appointed time, as I always like to arrive early for everything – ask my wife! This time, my punctuality paid dividends – we were directed across the huge courtyard and ushered through various doors and corridors. I was whisked off to an ante-room while the others were led into the splendid ballroom, set out with row upon row of red plush chairs, where the ceremony would take place. As they were among the first to arrive, it was almost empty. On asking where they should sit, they were told they could take seats right in the front row and so had a perfect view of the whole proceedings – I was thus able to justify being so early!

In fact, they saw more than I did, for I spent only a brief few moments in the presence of Her Majesty, while my family witnessed, at close hand, all kinds of notable people being honoured, including several Falklands war veterans, or, sadly in some cases, their widows. They also saw some knighthoods being bestowed with a kneeling-stool and sword, which they said was a very powerful and moving experience.

Meanwhile, I waited in the ante-room talking to a wide variety of people, all of whom, like myself, were to receive an honour of some sort. They came from all walks of life – some were important in the world of business or public service, while others, like myself, were ordinary citizens who had helped their local community in some way. But whatever their status, everyone was very friendly and we calmed each other's nerves while waiting for our moment of glory.

When my name was called, one equerry prodded me forward and then another halted my progress until the exact moment when I had to stand before the Queen and accept my medal. Another official held a small cushion on which the medal rested, and whispered something about me, as he did for everyone in turn. As Her Majesty picked up the medal and attached it to a small hook on my jacket, she graciously thanked me for sending her one of our Youth Orchestra records. Then she shook my hand and that was that! She was much smaller than I had imagined and looked even more so, standing next to some of her staff. Afterwards, outside, we had some official photographs taken and then all went for a celebratory meal and an evening at a theatre, which rounded off a memorable experience for us all.

In 1985 we had news from Hofheim that our old friend Klaus Giesen, who had helped us so much with our exchange visits, had died of a heart attack. We were all very sad, because by now we regarded him as a close personal friend. He had been very keen on church architecture and history in general, very knowledgeable on a wide range of subjects and altogether a most interesting person to know. He was delighted when Margaret began her first efforts at speaking to him in German. When he heard about our visit to the Royal Garden Party, and later my MBE investiture, he asked for a full account of both, which he translated for the Hofheimer Zeitung, the local newspaper. He was a great Anglophile, and delighted in learning new things about our history and customs.

It was about this time that I embarked on a new venture; I began to write a musical composition, which I eventually decided to call the *Celebration March*. It took me quite a long time, but I was able to use the knowledge I had built up from studying scores of all kinds – and my friends and family thought it sounded very good. I had intended it as an orchestral piece, and it was played once or twice with my orchestra and also the Town Band, but having heard it several times as an organ recital, I rather feel it is better suited to this. In fact, the very first time it ever had a public airing was at our son's first wedding in Chesterfield, when the organist was full of praise for my effort. I felt very flattered recently when one of my former pupils, and ex-orchestra member, Sharon Squibb (née Stuckey), asked permission to have it played at her wedding. Of course, I readily agreed. It was played by Mr Andrew Curtis, who has been a source of support to the orchestra on many occasions.

Times Were Starting to Change

Music, when soft voices die, vibrates in the memory
(Shelley)

In 1989 I received a letter from my old friend, Günter Powils, telling me that for several reasons, including health and family commitments, he had resigned as Chairman of the Akkordeon Orchester. He told me that our next visit would be arranged by his successor, Joachim Loos. When we began our exchanges Joachim was a teenager, but now, having recently married another of their members, Ulla, and having experienced a number of our exchange visits, he felt prepared – with another seasoned member, Dietmar Viertel – to take over the administration.

It was also about this time that we heard with great sorrow that our kind host and friend, Karl-Heinz Mock, had died – he had failed to recover from recent major heart surgery. This was a shock, as he had seemed so well on our last visit. Somehow the deaths of these two men – first Klaus Giesen and then Karl-Heinz Mock – seemed like the end of an era.

However, later that year, we enjoyed what was to be our last visit to Hofheim with myself as conductor. It was not quite the same in many ways, and the Akkordeon Orchester had a new conductor in place of Josef Dieser. There were also a few minor problems, although they did eventually get sorted out. For this visit, to avoid such a long journey across the Channel and overland, we had chosen to fly. With most of the party already through the airport's departure gate, one person's passport was found not to be in order. There was a great deal of anxiety and a little panic, but they rushed off to another terminal and managed to obtain a valid visitor's passport. Luckily we were in plenty of time! On the way back our coach to take us to the airport was very late and we only just managed to get our luggage checked through in time to get on the plane! Still, we all had a good time and it was lovely to see all our old friends and meet new ones.

The following year, 1990, was rather special because it was the 10th anniversary of the official twinning between our two towns. The Mayor of Hofheim, together with other officials, would be coming to Tiverton for special celebrations – and naturally the Akkordeon Orchester Hofheim wished to be a part of this, because it was also their 40th anniversary.

We decided that this would also be the last exchange visit that Margaret, Jeanne and I would arrange, as we had done it now for a long time and it was becoming increasingly difficult for us all. I wanted to think of a really nice gift to mark this special occasion. In the past we had tended to give just one item – perhaps a plaque or a book or a video – and receive something similar from them in return. It was impossible to share these with all the members but, on our last visit to Hofheim, each person had been given an individual gift of chocolates, and this seemed to me much better.

So, after much thought, we commissioned an order of 100 commemorative ceramic mugs, with our logo and theirs, one on each side. We had organised a big concert, which formed part of the official celebration of the Twinning, on June 16th at the Tiverton High School. It was a worthy finale to our series of exchanges and we performed in a packed hall before a distinguished audience of officials from both towns. At the end, the mugs were duly presented to our orchestra friends and to some of the officials, including their Mayor and ours. A few were sent back to Hofheim to be given to some of our old friends who could not be with us, while the remainder were distributed among our own members. The last one was given to Tiverton Museum. I hope everyone has taken great care of their mugs, because they must surely be collectors' items by now!

It was just about a year later that my great friend and colleague, Wilf Saunders, suffered the loss of his wife, Berys, who – despite a long and exhausting illness – had always cheerfully helped us in any way she could. She was, and indeed still is, greatly missed.

I decided, with a great deal of regret, that the time had come for me to lay down my baton, at least on a regular basis. I asked Wilf if he would be prepared to take over from me. He was reluctant at first, as he was still coming to terms with his loss of his wife – and his family understandably feared it might prove too big a commitment.

I received a few enquiries from various people who heard I was about to retire and thought they might like to take on the Orchestra. However, the first question each of them asked was "How much is the pay?" And I am afraid they soon lost interest when they discovered there was none, and never had been!

A concert at St Paul's Church with Miss Edna Rogers and the Heathcoat Junior School Choir — 1992

(Courtesy of Tiverton Gazette)

My Farewell Celebration Concert

Those who love the young best, stay young the longest

(E.Z. Friedenberg)

From 1991 until 1992 Wilf and I worked even more closely together, with myself still planning concerts and deciding on the music. I would rearrange the scores where necessary, while he would conduct some of the items and assist in making arrangements. He was, of course, no stranger to the Youth Orchestra, having been involved for so many years, but he was getting ready to take over from me as smoothly as possible – and I was getting ready for my big farewell concert, planned for May 1992.

The headmaster of Blundell's School, Mr John Rees, and the head of their music department, Andrew Barlow, once again offered us the use of the School Hall. I invited some of their music staff and pupils to join us and also got in touch with a number of past members, several of whom were able to return for this special occasion. I was also delighted that my daughter, Jeanne, who had given up playing with us some years ago, agreed to return to the percussion section in order to take part.

By the time all this was organised, I knew there would be about 100 players, with a good range of instruments and ability, so I felt confident that we would be able to put on a concert as good as any we had ever done. It would be a worthy finale to this long association with the Tiverton Youth Orchestra, which I had formed back in 1944.

Once again I invited Mr David Chivers to compère the event. Naturally, Christopher Martin was keen to make another special guest appearance and I asked a few former and current members to perform as soloists. We decided to donate any profits to the Save the Children Fund. This was not only because it is a very worthwhile cause, but also I knew that Sir Ian and Lady Amory actively supported this charity and it was a way of thanking them for all their kindness to us over the past years. I wrote to the charity's patron – Princess Anne, The Princess Royal – in the hope that she might come, as I heard she would possibly be in the West Country at about that time. She was not, alas, available, but we did receive a very nice letter from her personal secretary.

I also mentioned to some of our Hofheim friends about the coming concert, but did not offer an invitation, as I felt we could not cope with an official visit as well as the concert and I knew they were quite busy with their own engagements at that time.

I was very pleased to see that tickets were selling well. The afternoon rehearsal for all participants went quite smoothly – and so, on May 2nd, 1992, what I had entitled my 'Celebration Concert' took place. I was just a bit disappointed that I had not received any message of good wishes from Hofheim, as they were generally very thoughtful about this sort of thing. However, I had quite a few from other old friends who were unable to attend.

Blundell's School Hall was well filled as I took up my baton and commenced the concert with the National Anthem, followed by what had become our theme tune, *Hello Friends* by Josef Dieser.

David Chivers then read a selection of the letters I had received. He came to one of them and said, "I also have one here from the Hofheim Akkordeon Orchester," and he reached into his jacket pocket to bring out a piece of paper. I was so pleased to know they had not forgotten us after all. "But," continued David, "I don't think I'll read it. I'll let them speak for themselves."

And then, to my utter amazement, coming down the aisle towards me was Josef himself, with a few members of the Hofheim Orchester, carrying accordions! I was astonished and everyone must have seen by the expression on my face that I really had no idea that they were coming. It did explain a few things that had puzzled me; for example, I was told by my daughter that the gents' toilet in the corridor next to the school dining hall was out of order and I had to go and find another one behind the stage. They had all been hiding near there until the concert began and she was afraid I would spot them!

There were just six of their members, including Joachim Loos, Dietmar Viertel and Alfred Füller. We played *Hello Friends* once more with the accordions joining in and ended up with Josef and myself conducting it together.

After that bit of excitement I had to pull myself together and press on with the programme as planned – and with David continuing with the announcements, we managed to get back on track.

There were many of our old favourites among the pieces I had chosen and all the soloists performed exceptionally well. Amanda Kelly played the piano, Michael Purrington, the cello. Duets were performed by Gina Kelly and Sharon Clatworthy (flute), Bridget and Catherine Tosh (piano). Bridget Budge (contralto) and Sarah Heard (soprano) made their contributions with very different but equally memorable vocal solos. Of course, Christopher Martin not only enthralled the audience in his own inimitable way with his music, but caused a great deal of laughter as he recounted several of his favourite musical anecdotes. He also described conversations he claimed he regularly had with me, when I would phone him in Melbourne at 3 am, Australian time, wanting to know what the weather was like over there!

Christopher was accompanied at the piano by Heather Howell, the daughter of Wilf Saunders, and a very able musician in her own right. She was, of course, also a former member of the orchestra. It was very hard to choose my soloists, for there were others, equally talented, who would probably have liked to take part. I hope they understood that only the need to keep the length of the programme within reasonable limits prevented me from asking every one of them.

David read the letter from the Princess Royal's secretary and, after the interval, the six accordion players gave a short recital. A letter from their Mayor, Herr Rolf Felix, was read, together with a message from the rest of their members.

I played my violin for one of my favourite pieces – *Intermezzo* from *Cavalleria Rusticana* by Mascagni – and I noticed that several of our players were wiping away a few tears by the end. It is indeed a very moving melody.

We ended with a rousing version of Elgar's *Pomp and Circumstance March*, for which our son, John, (at David's suggestion) came out from the audience to join us in the percussion section. Faith Hill-King played the trumpet solo, and Bridget Budge, wearing a splendid gown, did justice to the vocal solo.

The whole concert was recorded for us on video by a local firm, MKG Video Productions, which made a wonderful souvenir of the occasion. At the end, I formally handed over my baton to my successor, Wilf Saunders.

Margaret and I at the buffet lunch at the Rugby Club — 1992

I did not want any lengthy presentations at the concert as there was to be a celebratory buffet lunch at the Rugby Club next day, but Sir Ian Amory gave a speech of thanks and Margaret and Jeanne were given flowers, presented by my granddaughter, Emma. She was only nine at the time and was rather overwhelmed by the occasion! I said a few words and invited any former members in the audience to stand up. I was very pleased to see many familiar faces from the past.

Next day, at the buffet lunch, a number of other former members put in an appearance. Margaret and Jeanne had commissioned a special, violin–shaped cake from one of them, Stella Tucker, which looked wonderful. Like many of my former members she is now married with a family.

The orchestra presented me with a wonderful souvenir – a silver-framed photograph of the whole orchestra and part of the audience taken from the balcony of the school hall the previous evening. And from Hofheim came a splendid basket of German delicacies, presented on their behalf by Joachim Loos.

You may recall that I mentioned finding a record of our Albert Hall concert at a jumble sale some time before, which I had bought for 10p. I told everyone about this and how sad I had been to find it like that, so we sold raffle tickets for it, raising another £30 or so to add to the proceeds of the concert. In due course a cheque for £1,000 was sent to the Save the Children Fund and I later received a handsome, framed certificate in acknowledgment.

Sharing a laugh with Wilf Saunders, the new TYO conductor, ready for a joint concert — 1994

(Courtesy of Express & Echo)

The Orchestra Carries On

There will be more songs – more songs tomorrow,
though it is not we who shall sing them
(From *Sword at Sunset*, by Rosemary Sutcliffe)

After this concert I was, of course, no longer responsible for planning the rehearsals, concerts etc. I had very mixed feeling about this. Part of me was a little relieved to be free, but for quite a long time I did miss making decisions and generally being in charge. In fact, in a way, I still miss it, though I know I no longer have the stamina to carry on. Wilf was very careful to include me in all kinds of discussions and I knew I was always welcome at any rehearsals. Occasionally, when he was ill or away, I even took a rehearsal again, and he often asked me to choose a piece to prepare and conduct at a concert, so I was eased out very gently, which was much nicer for me than a sudden breakaway. I appreciated his tact and thoughtfulness in this respect.

He was quite keen to continue the contact with Hofheim if at all possible and so, in 1996, he decided to take the Orchestra over there once more and asked if I would go with them. At first I said no, as I felt my days of hectic foreign exchange visits were well and truly over. Also, I did not want to seem to intrude on his first visit as the new conductor. However, he begged me to reconsider and finally I agreed, but decided we would fly from Bristol as the others would be going by coach – too long a journey for me. We wrote to Marianne Mock to ask if she would be able to put us up and she readily agreed.

It was lovely to see so many of our old friends once more and we were all given a wonderful welcome. The programme for the visit was similar to our previous ones; concerts in the two retirement homes and a big one in the Town Hall.

This time Margaret and I did not go on all the various trips arranged for the members. We had been to most of them before and we were not really needed, as there were plenty of adults to help with the group. We were otherwise entertained by Marianne and her family, including her daughter, Heidi, and her husband, Josef Freml, who was very ill and has, sadly, since died; their two sons, Matthias and Tomas, whom we had watched growing up over the years; Hans-Jürgen, my very first contact; and Marianne's good friend, Franz.

They were all very kind to us. We had several invitations to 'kaffee und kuchen' with various people we had met before. One evening Marianne invited several of the original organisers of the Akkordeon Orchester for the evening and we had a splendid time together, reminiscing over our past exchanges and long friendships.

Josef Dieser, who died in September 1996

For the orchestra's main concert, I had been rehearsing my own composition, *Celebration March*, with them for some weeks and we were also going to play *Hello Friends* as usual. We had heard that Josef Dieser was very ill and I doubted if I would meet him at all during our visit. As the concert began I looked around, but did not see him. However, at the end of my piece, suddenly there he was, walking down the aisle clapping vigorously as he came up to shake my hand and praise the music. I was very moved. When the concert was over, I presented him with a copy of my composition and gave him permission to use it as he wished. That was the last time we saw him, for only a short time later we heard that he had died.

The only thing that marred this lovely visit was a silly accident on the day before my return; I slipped down some marble steps and cracked a bone in my ankle. I was wheeled through the huge Frankfurt Airport in style by a very pretty stewardess and given VIP treatment all the way home, including several free miniatures of Scotch whisky – for the pain, you understand!

Chris Martin

Over the next few years, I still attended some rehearsals, though not on a regular basis. The last big concert with which I was involved took place in 1999. Chris Martin came over once more as guest soloist and I played in the orchestra. I was very pleased that my granddaughter, Emma, also took part. She was fast becoming a seasoned performer herself as a mezzo-soprano, being taught by Mrs Marilyn Felix and regularly competing and winning prizes in regional music festivals. She had sung solos with us on several previous occasions and now she and Chris had a chance to hear each other's performances. I could not help remembering her very first public solo, when she stood up and sang for the old people in Germany, at the age of four! The third soloist that evening was Gordon Hills, who is often seen busking for charity in Tiverton town centre with his euphonium. The whole evening was a great success and everyone did very well.

In memory of Berys, Wilf asked that the proceeds should go to the Exeter Leukaemia Fund, a group set up to help research and also support families affected by this illness – and we were delighted that we raised £865 for this good cause.

This was to be Wilf's last big event with the Tiverton Youth Orchestra. At the end of 2000, ill health caused him to hand over the baton to yet another conductor, Mr John Fitton, a local school music teacher, who later married one of our members, Catherine Tosh. Trevor Chilcott, at the age of 70, decided, also for health reasons, that it was time to bow out. He had been a member for 56 years – not a bad record of loyalty! At a concert, which formed part of the Tiverton Spring Festival programme that year, presentations were made to Wilf and Trevor, for all they had done for the orchestra over many years.

I would like to think that the Tiverton Youth Orchestra, which I founded all those years ago, will continue to give encouragement to young players and pleasure to their audiences for many more years. I hope there will always be someone willing to give freely of his or her time to carry on showing young people that classical music can also be good fun and to give them and their audiences something worth hearing, no matter how tastes and fashions may change.

We must have raised many thousands of pounds for good causes over 50 years and I hope, too, that this is a tradition that will continue. It is always good to know that you have helped others.

There are so many people to thank, to remember with affection, that I cannot possibly name them all. Apart from our members, we had many regular supporters who attended our concerts most faithfully, helped us with fund-raising and were generally there for us. I should like to express my thanks to every one of them – if your name was not mentioned in this book, I apologise – there were just too many of you!

Still, I hope this book will bring back happy memories to you all.

A complete list
of those who took part in the concert at

The Royal Albert Hall

April 15th 1977

Violins

Jacqueline Attwood	Tracey Attwood	Irvine Bendelow
Bridget Budge	Tina Butt	Trevor Chilcott
Martin Chilcott	David Chilcott	Agnes Dyson
Heidi Fitzpatrick	Catherine Furse	Brian Greenslade
Joanne Greenslade	Nicola Goddard	Andrew Hutton
Kate Jewell	Teresa Lockyer	Sarah Manaton
Christopher Martin	Caroline Morris	Helen Morris
Maureen Rendell	Patrick Rudall	Heather Saunders
Wilfred Saunders	Sharon Scoble	Alan Smale
Melanie Stain	Bruno Stuart	Reginald Tayler
Claire Taylor	Emma Thompson	Elizabeth Thorne
Pansy Tucker	Andrew Vickery	Silagh Voce
Philip Williams	Penny Wood	

Flutes

Jennifer Hill	Susan Radford	Anne Rendell
Susan Russell	Bridget Sweetland	Susan Walter
Susan Webber		

French Horns

Alison Gunn	Ruth Wotton

Percussion

Simon Clarke	John Davey	Jonathan Haddock
Jeanne Kellow	Michael Soundy	Keith Stone

Piano

Eileen Pengelly	Marjorie Smale

Trombones

Gordon Hills	Ian Hills	Paul Joslin
Ian Pengelly	Graham Pillivant	Steven Pillivant

Trumpets

Sandra Bryant, Paula Diggle, Sallianne Diggle
Jeremy Hann, Michael Hawkins, Christopher Petticrew
Stephen Russell, Stewart Taylor, Ronald Voce
Peter Waite

Violas

Eric Chilcott, Vivien Field, Theresa Foster
Felicity Gardiner, Simon Parton

Cellos

Leslie Balaam, Juliet Foster, Alan Furse
Stephen Mudge, Andrew Rendell

Double Basses

George Dyson, Christopher Edworthy

Oboes

Nicholas Cornish, Beverley Hill

Bassoons

Alexander Haines, Alice Wall

Clarinets

Russell Ayre, Deborah Barlow, Richard Chilcott
Jill Cowley, Helen Grant, Karen Greening
Judith Greensmith, Susan Hawkins, Alison Howard
Janet Piercey, David Saunders, Catherine Walter
Susan Walter, Carol Webber, Susan Whatley

Saxaphone

Paul Bryant

Tuba

Paul Matthews

Soloists and Accompanists

Rosemary Davis, Dorothy Dey, Ian Gorman
Gordon Hills, Stephen Russell, Heather Saunders
Derek Stone, John Whitechurch

Announcers

Robert Lockyer, Brian Reade

Soloists at Various Concerts

Over the years many members have performed as soloists at Tiverton Youth Orchestra concerts. I have done my best, with the aid of old programmes, to include as many as possible in the following list:

Jacki Attwood	Russell Ayre	Gemma Best
Natalie Best	Angela Blackwell	Bridget Budge
Rachel Buy	Nicola Cardwell	Nick Carter
Julia Chilcott	Richard Chilcott	Sharon Clatworthy
Rosemary Davis	Clare Felix	John Fewings
Teresa Foster	Keith Green	Tracey Harman
Sarah Head	Reg Heal	Faith Hill-King
Gordon Hills	Rachael Hoinville	Roland Huish
Deborah Hunter	Emma Kellow	Amanda Kelly
Georgina Kelly	Christopher Martin	Stephen Mudge
Jane Parkhouse	Gerald Petticrew	Janet Piercey
Graham Pillivant	Georgina Pratt	Alison Purrington
Andrew Rendell	Fred Rendell	Hannah Reynolds
Anna Rufey	Stephen Russell	Heather Saunders
Lynn Sowden	Melanie Stain	Claire Taylor
Andrew Tosh	Marjorie Tucker	Judith Webber
Helen Wilson		

Postscript

by Christopher Martin

My association with Youth Orchestras and Youth Music Camps has without doubt been some of the most rewarding experiences in my professional life. In today's world, youth orchestras abound and are, almost without exception, conducted by professional musicians. This is what makes the Tiverton Youth Orchestra particularly remarkable.

It was founded and conducted by Ronald Davey, who was not a professional musician. Yet for more than 50 years he inspired a town and imparted to countless young people a love of music and the realisation of the enormous pleasure it can give to people, while at the same time being a lot of fun.

I was privileged to be the first leader of the Tiverton Youth Orchestra and through the years have remained conscious of that privilege – always very happy to join with it under Ron's direction whenever circumstances made it possible. Of all the orchestras I have been associated with, both Youth and Professional, the TYO is closest to my heart. The happy memories are vivid and, along with the many youngsters who were members, I am deeply grateful for the experience.

Christopher J. Martin 2001